Critical concepts in management and organization studies

palgrave critical management studies

Critical concepts in management and organization studies

Peter Stokes

Professor of Sustainable Management, Marketing and
Tourism, University of Chester

palgrave
macmillan

First published 2011 by
PALGRAVE MACMILLAN

Palgrave Macmillan in the UK is an imprint of Macmillan Publishers Limited, registered in England, company number 785998, of Houndmills, Basingstoke, Hampshire RG21 6XS.

Palgrave Macmillan in the US is a division of St Martin's Press LLC, 175 Fifth Avenue, New York, NY 10010.

Palgrave Macmillan is the global academic imprint of the above companies and has companies and representatives throughout the world.

Palgrave® and Macmillan® are registered trademarks in the United States, the United Kingdom, Europe and other countries.

ISBN 978–0–230–01974–4 paperback

This book is printed on paper suitable for recycling and made from fully managed and sustained forest sources. Logging, pulping and manufacturing processes are expected to conform to the environmental regulations of the country of origin.

A catalogue record for this book is available from the British Library.

A catalog record for this book is available from the Library of Congress.

10   9   8   7   6   5   4   3   2   1
20 19 18 17 16 15 14 13 12 11

Printed and bound in China

To Emma, Joel and Ellie – who are everything and the reason why – wishing you health and happiness always.
'As long as there is a sky over the Earth' – Deuteronomy 11:2

כִּימֵי הַשָּׁמַיִם, עַל-הָאָרֶץ

Contents

Introduction

The aim of this text is to provide entry points to, and initial understandings of, the broad area termed **Critical Management Studies** (CMS). The need for this text emerges from experiences and observations by the author and academic colleagues which have pointed up a number of recurrent issues that impact on students:

- The relative youth of CMS as an academic domain (or domains) means that student-orientated writings, such as textbooks, are a relatively recent occurrence in the field and there is a need for an accessible handbook that provides basic initial insights and links across CMS terminology;
- The difficulty many students find in approaching CMS-related literature and writings due to the challenging language in which they are couched. The recognition that, like much academic writing, CMS materials, and especially journal articles, are written as much for a peer academic group as for students and this may not be the most amenable format for student appreciation or understanding of the sphere;
- The recognition that students often undertake CMS-oriented or informed modules as *part* of a course rather than CMS approaches representing all course content (– typical module titles might be, for example, *Critical Perspectives on Organizations*, *Alternative Perspectives on Organization and Management*, *Contemporary Approaches to Organizations*, *Contemporary Issues in Management and Organization Studies*, *Social and Organization Theory*, *Critical Management Research* to indicate but a few). This means they can encounter, sometimes in quite a contrasting and abrupt way, approaches to looking at organization and

management which are often quite a **radical** change to the theory they have hitherto encountered and there is a need for texts that assist in such transitions.

CMS is a rich and complex area that draws its inspiration and analyses from a lengthy catalogue of materials and sources, including, by way of example, existentialism, **Critical Theory**, **postmodernism**, **poststructuralism**, **feminism**, **deconstructionism** and **critical realism**. Since its inception there has been no shortage of writing and commentary employing CMS stances. In many ways this output has been comprised of recognizable phases of development for bodies of literature whereby, what commenced in CMS as a small number of incipient indicative texts and articles published around the early 1990s (drawing primarily on ideas of **Critical Theory** and **postmodernism**) has now rapidly mushroomed into myriad journal articles, and a wide range of texts and forms (see Clegg, Kornberger, Carter and Rhodes, 2006; Phillips, 2006; Adler, Forbes and Willmott, 2007; Adler, 2008; Cooke, 2008; Stookey, 2008; Voronov, 2008 for a more comprehensive account of these developments). In more recent years, and of particular interest to the present text, CMS-centric and CMS-focused readers and student textbooks have started to appear more regularly and these are a welcome addition for students seeking to appreciate and understand some of the issues in the field (see by way of illustration: Alvesson and Spicer, 2010; Clegg, Kornberger and Pitsis, 2008; Grey and Willmott, 2005; Knights and Willmott, 2007; Linstead, Fulop and Lilley, 2009; Fineman, Gabriel and Sims, 2010).

All of these developments have gone hand in hand with the growing strength of CMS-associated conferences (for example, the *International Critical Management Studies Conference* (CMS), *European Group on Organizational Studies* (EGOS) and the *Standing Conference on Organizational Symbolism* (SCOS)), and the inauguration of professorial chairs and university business and management departments that are essentially CMS-inspired. Perhaps one of the unavoidable, however uncomfortable, paradoxical and consequential **truths** for a **radical** CMS is that the domain is to some greater or lesser extent becoming institutionalized (see **institution**) and is beginning to receive some of the reflections and critiques that it originally levelled at more **normative** and **mainstream** approaches.

Given the diverse spectrum of philosophical and **ideological** positions espoused by many of those committed and involved in the CMS field (half-jokingly self-styled as 'critters'), this history has not necessarily been an easy one. In some regards, many CMS critiques have been wary of coming up with *direct* suggested 'solutions' to organizational challenges and problems for fear that they might, in turn, be peer-criticized for being **representationalist**, essentialist, simplistic and even *naïve*. In other words, the issue of practical impact, usefulness and **performativity** of CMS has constituted a particularly difficult debate within the field (see Willmott, 2006; Cooke, 2008; Spicer, Alvesson and Kärreman, 2009 for illustrative further expansion on these discussions). In essence, translation of CMS ideas and concepts has sometimes seemed problematic to adapt or integrate into workplaces. Perhaps one of the reasons for this is the complex and occasionally obtuse sociological language in which many CMS texts and arguments are couched. Peer-reviewed academic journals are, perhaps quite rightly, viewed as a place where academic communities present, argue and challenge ideas and beliefs. However, for many students working their way through these texts can be a daunting prospect. Indeed, often the reality is that they are written not for students but for academic peers and there is frequently a reluctance to move away from complex **language** for fear of peer criticism or reproach. Many students undertake a business or organization and management studies programme and suddenly find themselves plunged into a world of complex sociological terminology. The concepts are often abstract, difficult to grasp or relate to their own **realities**. In the present text, the intention is not to patronize students nor to devalue or deride the work of academic writers and scholarship. Rather, within the overall development of CMS, it is arriving timely to create teaching and learning materials that will support and complement existing and evolving texts.

As mentioned earlier, CMS-informed teaching may sometimes constitute part of a modular or course experience. For example, it is quite possible that students receive lectures in business economic theory or a conventional and normative presentation of, say, marketing or accounting. This may well be combined with CMS-style or informed modules and this can produce a confusion or tension in students' minds. As such they may be coming to CMS through a hybrid form of experience. Some may say this is the essence of higher education experience and the challenge and joy is to read, study and unravel that complexity to a resolution for individual understanding. This is indeed valid but a text that provides a handrail and an initial foothold on ideas and topics will be a valuable aid to that process.

In summary, it is the aim and purpose of this text to assist students and lecturers in addressing the above issues. As CMS has tentatively moved towards texts that have begun to render it more accessible, it has trodden carefully to avoid charges of over-simplifying or 'dumbing down'. Due to the pressures and tensions detailed above, some of these texts have nevertheless produced very strong (some might even say disingenuous and ill-founded) reactions from some corners of the CMS community. In spite of such concerns, there is nevertheless need for a brief reference text – one that students can have by their side simply to read a quick overview on a few related terms in CMS. This book provides them with an entry, a starting point. It does not try to be the rounded or comprehensive response – that is not its job. It is a quick reference guide that will get students started and gain access to the 'world(s)' of CMS writing.

In terms of format, the text of the book is by its very nature and attitude neural and **rhizomatic** that is as terms are employed in the entries, the reader has the possibility of moving from one entry to another exploring the ideas presented and thus building up a picture that suits his or her own appreciation of the critical sphere. Moreover, the text does not seek to present itself as a complete solution. Rather, again in **rhizomatic** terms, it is a hub within a wider neural network of knowledge providing students with manageable entry points to more in-depth and specific readings. With regard to the readings indicated at the foot of each entry, many of these of course serve the role to provide more information on the topic word. In addition, they also provide useful illustrations of the word being employed in varying context (s) which is valuable for a rounded understanding of terms to be developed. Moreover, it is clearly not intended that the text will remain static and unchanging. Revisions of the text will remain conscious of its own development (its historicity – or its own progressive and gradual historical development) in relation to the evolutions and gradual transformations in the CMS field(s). Above all, it is therefore the hope and intention that both students and tutors will find this book of value in developing their studies further.

Professor Peter Stokes
Chester Business School,
University of Chester.

Acknowledgements

The gestation and production of this text have been challenging and involved the need to overcome a number of unforeseeable setbacks and obstacles on the journey. This would not have been possible without the constant support and encouragement of a number of people.

I would like to thank heartfully my publisher at Palgrave Macmillan, Ursula Gavin and her colleague Ceri Griffiths. Without the valuable and helpful conversations and support that Ursula provided, it is difficult to imagine that the project would have arrived at this successful conclusion. I would also like to thank many other colleagues who offered wise words and good humour along the way, in particular, Professor Clare Brindley, Professor Alistair McCulloch, Dr Cynthia Dereli, Dr Scott Lawley, Dr Wes Harry, Dr Mitch Larson, Professor Nigel Holden, Dr Frank Worthington and Professor John Wilson.

My wife, Emma, and children, Joel and Ellie, and my wider family and friends in Southport, Liverpool, London and the Midlands have also lived the writing of the book. I want to say thank you to them for their patience and incisive humour which help us all to stay 'grounded' and receptive to the world. I can only say that I will endeavour to make the writing of future books less 'visible'.

Finally, to Mum and Dad who left us a long time ago and would have loved to have seen this happen.

Tikkun Olam – Repair of the World

Professor Peter Stokes
Chester Business School,
University of Chester.

Entries

Actor Network Theory

Actor Network Theory (ANT) is a theoretical approach that attempts to map and understand the relationship and interplay between physical or material objects and concepts. For example, an organization is composed of many *physical artefacts* including buildings, furniture, vehicles, computer systems and so on and so forth. At the same time there are many principles, concepts, notions, ideas and technologies that are generated, disseminated, communicated and shared. ANT is interested in trying to explain how these aspects operate as an overall whole. In other words, this holistic view is often referred to as a **material-semiotic** method (i.e. relating to signs, **language** and **discourse**) which means that it considers the symbiotic relationship between people, things and ideas.

ANT employs the term 'actants' which can refer to human *or* inanimate objects between whom, for the purposes of ANT, there is no distinction. Both humans and objects are capable of actions and they have equal potential for impact on other things and people. In this way, ANT believes that it is important not to draw clear **delineations** between people, technology and objects. The most important distinction for ANT is the actual *network of relations* that is generated and any element of the network might be responsible for this.

Key writers in the field of ANT include the French sociologists Michel Callon (1945–) and Bruno Latour (1947–) and the United Kingdom-based academic John Law. A central tenet of ANT thinking is that such systems or **material-semiotic** states are not static or fixed but rather are in a perpetual state of forming and reforming. The people or 'actors' within such systems are the key activists that make this happen. Without their presence and continuing intervention the **material-semiotic** would not continue to function and would begin to disintegrate. This also means that there is no particular clear or self-evident order to such systems. They are perpetually and continuously made and remade by activity and action. Hence, the unpredictable organic nature of such systems means that that they are very rhizomatic (see **rhizome**). Equally it can be seen how ideas of **social constructionism** play a role in ANT influenced settings as actants make, and remake, sense and meaning in the changing contexts and circumstances.

ANT has grown into a complex field but its primary concerns revolve around concepts of: *Problematization*, *Interressment*, *Enrolment* and *Mobilization* (Latour, 1987). In other words, this can be understood in order as: issues of identifying problems (and whether or not there is merit in attempting to build a network), engaging and recruiting actors (and convincing them of their roles and the merits of the issues and case) and assembling interest groups around the core actors (i.e. the rolling out of the influence of the group). Within ANT terminology *mediators* play an important role driving forward actions and creating change and differences in the network. Intermediaries simply pass the power on, transposing it to another part of the system. However, it should be noted that it may be impossible to know who is the most influential or significant actor until the end of a phase or playing out of interactions.

The validity and utility of ANT have been challenged in recent years and even commentators such as its proponent, Latour, have on occasion shown an ambivalent attitude towards the theory (Linstead, 2004: 175).

Key Words:

Language, Material-semiotic, Rhizome, Semiotic, Social Constructionism.

References

Alcadipani and Hassard (2010); Latour (1987); Linstead (2004).

Aesthetics

Aesthetics is a field of philosophy that is concerned with the concept, study and creation of beauty. Aesthetics, therefore, invokes discussion on a wide range of related issues including art, taste, appreciation, pleasure and the sensory means people employ in order to engage with these issues. Aesthetics is frequently discussed in association with the world of art and, in particular, the philosophy of art. Overall, aesthetics is generally considered to be a challenging topic leading to complex methodological and philosophical debates.

The notion of aesthetic 'beauty' as a possible inherent quality of an object or phenomenon is a recurrent debate in aesthetics. The German philosopher Immanuel Kant (1724–1804) suggested that beauty is innate in objects and that everyone is likely to recognize and agree on a particular beauty. Subsequent contemporary debates have questioned whether beauty is actually central or integral to aesthetics at all and, if it is not, what stands or operates in its place in the aesthetic realm (Massumi, 2002). Furthermore, a key issue in relation to aesthetics is how judgements on aesthetics are formed. Taste, and the question of what constitutes taste, is often considered the result of education and exposure to a particular set of cultural values.

Contemporary understandings of aesthetics have increasingly acknowledged the notion that personal and individual interpretations and perspectives play a significant role in forming aesthetic judgements. In this frame of reference, aesthetics has been embraced by **Critical Management Studies** (CMS) and critical approaches as a potentially fruitful area to consider in relation to organization and management studies. Particularly significant in these commentaries has been the work of Antonio Strati (1992) who has considered the concept of beauty in relation to organizational life as a whole, and with particular focus on issues of rites, **rituals** and **narratives**. Further analyses on aesthetics in these contexts show how art, dance, movement, music, fashion, **narrative**, theatre, craft, **voice**, support of the arts, and the internal and external appearance and image of organizations can be seen to play a role. In relation to more **mainstream** or **normative** approaches issues of aesthetics have not been necessarily explicitly surfaced and might be seen as being adequately discussed within, for example, marketing, design, PR or corporate reputation disciplinary areas of organization studies. However, many of these accounts tend to be **managerialist**, **reductionist** and **representationalist** in that they seek to understand and embrace aesthetic issues only in so far as they can contribute to organizational performance targets and profits. In this way, the sphere of aesthetics is commodified (see **commodification**) and it has been suggested that before a field of aesthetics can be appropriately considered it will be necessary to strip away establishment and institutional **appropriation** of aesthetics (Adorno, 1997). Critical approaches contrast considerably with mainstream approaches to aesthetics which are more concerned with the sociological and psychological impacts and interplay of aesthetic issues with organizations. An illustration of this is the concept of *aesthetic labour* – concerning the roles and impacts of the appearances of employees and individuals in work and organizational contexts has received a great deal of attention (see Witz, Warhurst and Nickson, 2003; Warhurst and Nickson, 2007). Within such commentaries it is possible to see bodies (see **body**) as something made or 'produced' in whole or in part by organizations and organizational life and consequently as something conceived and/or perceived as ugly, beautiful or aesthetically pleasing or displeasing.

Key Words:

Aesthetic Labour, Beauty, Narrative, Taste, Pleasure, Voice.

References

Adorno (1997); Hancock (2005); Linstead and Hopfl (2000); Mack (2008); Massumi (2002); Minahan and Wolfram-Cox (2007); Strati (1992); Warhurst and Nickson (2007); Witz, Warhurst and Nickson (2003).

Agency (adjective: agentic)

Agency concerns processes and experiences relating to a person, or a group of people charged and capable of carrying out actions in the role or capacity of an agent. In a popular sense, agents are seen as individuals or organizations that carry out action and tasks on behalf of other people, groups or organizations. Everyday examples of agency include travel, insurance and estate agents. In contemporary organizational life, managing or working for a company is a typical everyday example of fulfilling some form of agency role – individuals undertake tasks with, and on behalf of, others. In classical or **normative** organization theory, one of the most important groups is the managing directorate of a public company who act as agents for the shareholders. They have the remit and responsibility to manage the company in the most effective manner possible so as to protect and improve the capital investment of the shareholders. This is of course legalistically accurate; however, this perspective alone does not portray the potential complexity surrounding discussions on agency. From a **Critical Management Studies** (CMS) perspective, agency is inextricably bound up with issues of **knowledge**, **power** and **resistance** and their attendant cultural, **identity**, moral and ethical implications (see **morality** and **ethics**).

Within management and organization and wider social theory, agency points at the observation that people have freedom to act and *choices* to make in relation to their actions. This means that they can undertake actions that might be determined as having 'good' or 'bad' effects depending on the cultural, moral, political or ethical context and point of view taken (see **culture**, **moral** and **politics**). Nevertheless, agency does not imply that people are totally, and at all times, free to act as they wish and in this vein Giddens (1979) made an important contribution by examining agency in relation to **structure** (see **structuration**). He considered how **structure** produces actions and, in turn, actions create structures impacting on individuals and organizations. By way of illustration, the founding of a new government department will almost certainly lead to the department developing and introducing a series of initiatives. Reciprocally, a series of events or the roll out of these plans and actions may, consequently, lead to new departments and organizations being set up. It is therefore very difficult to separate out the interplay of action and structure – individuals and organizations produce, **reproduce** structure and yet are limited by structure in turn. In effect, while having the ability to create given structures or situations they are equally limited and constrained by those very structures. This runs counter to a dualistic (see **dualism**) view of agency in which action and structure are seen as separate from each other with the agent simply carrying out actions for the other party. Within philosophical traditions, in particular those pertaining to Marx and Hegel, agency is viewed more as a collective or societal project with a strong sense of historical identity and trajectory (see **capitalism**) rather than being comprised solely of individual actions.

Key Words:

Action, Choice, Dualism, Identity, Narrative, Power, Resistance, Reproduction, Structure.

References

Caldwell (2007); Giddens (1979); Kallinikos (2009).

Alienation

Alienation is the emergence of a sense of separation (in contrast to affinity and affiliation) between people, groups, tasks, roles or entities. Alienation, therefore, is concerned with issues of distancing or remoteness.

The concept of alienation is a recurrent theme in much critical commentary. Various forms of **agency** may produce effects of alienation. For **Critical Management Studies** (CMS), this is, for example, particularly the case where **managers** are considered to be operating in a **managerialist** manner that is felt to be oppressive or non-emancipatory (see **emancipation**) for **others**. Consequently, individuals or groups may feel as if they have been dislocated, isolated or excluded from particular identities (see **identity**). A typical illustration of this experience might be where a person's role is forcibly reconfigured and deskilled as part of an organizational restructuring. Where settings which are over-controlled or regulated are in evidence it is also possible that a condition of *anomie* might result as a consequence. Anomie is a reaction that can occur where over-regulated environments paradoxically produce reactions of heightened non-compliance or non-alignment. For individuals or groups who become alienated a condition of 'otherness' (see **other**), wherein identities (often negative) are imposed on them, may be a consequence.

Alienation has been extensively examined in relation to certain forms of managing and organizing particularly in connection with manufacturing and contemporary service contexts. **Fordism** and Fordist ways of structuring work (see **structure**) have been argued as having potential detrimental effects on worker **identity**, **autonomy** and **emancipation** (Braverman, 1974). In such settings, individuals struggle to comply with the standardized approaches and structures and the simplified and repetitious work tasks. An example of this would be working on a production line or in a call centre doing the same tasks hour after hour and day after day. As a consequence, a person may begin to lose his or her sense of individual worth and identity whilst, at the same time, not finding consolation or salvation within the larger corporate entity and its procedures. This process may well produce various forms of **resistance** by, and alternative identities in, the alienated parties. The field of **Labour Process Theory** has dedicated a considerable amount of debate to these issues and situations (see: *inter alia* Thompson, 2003, 2007).

Key Words:

Agency, Emancipation, Fordism, Identity, Labour Process Theory, Managerialism, Other, Resistance, Structure.

References

Braverman (1974); Cremin (2010); Johnsen and Gudmand-Høyer (2010); Johnson (2006); Thompson (2003, 2007).

Appropriation

Appropriation is the act of taking possession of something. It is particularly used where the person appropriating something does not really have the right to take over or take ownership of the object. In **Critical Management Studies** (CMS) texts the term 'appropriation' is employed to point at ways in which objects, ideas, concepts, symbols and meanings (see **symbolism** and **meaning**) which are originally part of another group are absorbed or assimilated by particular individuals, groups or organizations. An illustration of this includes when somebody deems to speak on behalf of another person, not allowing him or her to express his or her own view or even distorting them. This constitutes an appropriation of **voice**. Appropriation can have a wide range of impacts and effects on the individuals involved and is evidently bound up with issues and dynamics surrounding **power** and who, at any given point in time, is holding it.

It should also be noted that the term 'appropriation' is also historically associated with Marxist philosophy (see **Marxism** and **Capitalism**) and relates to Marx's observation that capitalists appropriate, or commandeer, the surplus produced by labour and do not remunerate them for it.

Key Words:

Take Over, Commandeer, Marxism, Meaning, Power, Symbolism, Voice.

References

Riad (2008); Slutskaya and De Cock (2008); Willmott (2010).

Authority

The notion of authority involves ideas of having the right or possessing a legitimacy to take particular decisions and actions. These rights may well allow the person(s) with authority to direct or control the actions of others. Of course, it is necessary for others to consent, albeit with commitment or reluctance, to be subjected to this authority. In any event, compliance of any degree does not prevent people from engaging in acts of resistance against the authority. This is important for critical approaches which recognize that authority exists, and may need to be practised, but would seek that the exercise of that authority to be done in, and for, a democratic or emancipatory (see **emancipation**) manner.

It is important to distinguish authority from **power**. Power is more concerned with the physical or coercive capacity to direct somebody even though the person directing might not have the right or legitimacy (i.e. authority) to do so. However, we might refer to some systems of directing and decision-making as 'authoritarian' in the sense of 'dictatorial' and in contrast to, for example, democratic (i.e. where, in principle, every individual has a **voice**). Equally, **power** and influence may be rooted in an individual's charisma and the degree to which people are won over by an individual's personality.

In many contemporary societies, authority often derives from function not privilege. In other words, it is the office or role that carries the rank and associated authority. This contrasts, for example, with a situation where a person belongs to a particular self-appointed or inheriting elite through which he or she automatically exercises certain forms of authority (i.e. the aristocracy or the monarchy). This is an important idea particularly developed by Weber who identified, and was concerned about, new *rational-legal* forms of authority emerging in novel bureaucratic (see **bureaucracy**) **structures** and organizational forms at the turn of the twentieth century. Thus a 'manager' has the right to manage invested in the role to which he or she is appointed – and not because they are a particular person or individual. Similarly, this idea is carried out in other spheres such as the military where a soldier salutes the officer's uniform and rank, and not the person who wears it. Weber also outlined three types of authority: *charismatic authority* – where individuals find they can hold power and influence based on their personality; *traditional authority* – derived from historical legacies such as, for example, noble or aristocratic inheritance; *rational authority* – which was the new emergent form Weber closely examined (see **bureaucracy** and **rationality**).

The possibility and reality of the exercise of excessive behaviour in relation to power and authority have been the focus of a number of important and striking historical episodes. One such evident tragic experience was the emergence of the Nazi regime of the Third Reich. In the wake of this, Theodor Adorno of the post-war Frankfurt School suggested that authoritarian behaviour was likely to be associated with prejudice and racism (Adorno et al., 1950) (see **Critical Theory**). Moreover, in a controversial set of experiments, Stanley Milgram showed how formal authority figures within a fake scientific experiment coerced individuals to take questionable and unethical actions that appeared to inflict dangerous levels of pain on people concealed behind a screen (Milgram, 1974).

Key Words:

Bureaucracy, Charisma, Emancipation, Power, Resistance, Structure, Voice.

References

Adorno, Frenkel-Brunswick, Levinson, and Sandford (1950); Casey (2004); Higgins and Tamm-Hallström (2007); Milgram (1974).

Body

To think of a body may immediately conjure up images of mass and solidity. 'Body' can be couched statically as a container and receptacle or alternatively, it might be viewed kinetically as a vessel, a vehicle for journeying. Bodies span the human, animate and inanimate. In contemporary critical debate bodies have become an important aspect of discussions on, among other things, **gender**, consumerism, environmentalism, advertising and religious **politics**. The body has become recognized as an important site where meaning is created and processed. Bodies are linked to senses and minds. Aesthetically, bodies can be simultaneously ugly and beautiful based on the function of constructions made of, and about, them (see **aesthetics**). Bodies, individual or corporate, may be magnificent or deplorable and pitiful – putrid and decrepit, corpse-like. Even empires, corporate and military, decline sooner or later. Bodies, animate or inanimate, may have longevity but they are almost never immortal. Growth, transformation and decay are inevitable. Bodies incorporate and reproduce beliefs, values and culture(s). Inanimate objects and entities also have these aspects because they are ascribed by human **gaze.** Body and bodies are thus central to human thinking and hence unavoidably core to the fields of organization and management (in both academic and **lived experience** terms). We make sense of the world by transposing and investing the human body and corporal forms in and over non-human objects (see **sense-making**). In the case of animate objects we conjure up scenarios among animals that play out human emotions and sense-making. For example, nature programmes are furnished with commentaries that talk to, and take, the viewer through animal behaviour as if they were human (see the discussions led by Professor Rene Ten Bos on this issue).

Organization theory frequently analyses the company and the corporate body as a body-like organism. The directorate constitute the head, the middle-management torso – connected to the head facilitates the rank and file limbs. Companies are also said to possess **culture(s)** – corporate cultures. They are sentient and feel pain and joy at the response of markets, employee success and strikes. The personification and generation of body-related metaphors in relation to organization is a common feature of a range of both critical and **normative** commentaries. In the contemporary era, the conceptualization of the body has been seriously challenged particularly in relation to medical developments for example cloning, cybernetics, transplant and the discovery of life-essences of DNA.

Key Words:

Culture, Gaze, Gender, Identity, Lived Experience, Normative, Organization, Politics.

References

Ball (2005); Böhm and Batta (2010); Cooper (2010); Foucault (1963, 1975/1979, 1976, 1984a, 1984b); Hassard, Holliday and Willmott (2000); Phillips and Rippin (2010); Slutskaya and De Cock (2008).

Boundary (plural: boundaries)

The notion of boundaries is a common theme in critical approaches to management and organization. A boundary usually indicates the limits of a domain or area encompassed by the confines of the boundary. Moreover, a boundary can also operate in a number of more complex ways. It can separate one entity from another entity. In so doing it potentially produces 'othering' (see **other**) effects with 'other(s)' enclosed within the boundary or outside it. However, it is important not to think of boundaries as simply physical entities or artefacts. Boundaries can be created in a wide range of manners – for example, spatially (to do with space and place – see **spatial**), linguistically (to do with **language** and **discourse**) and temporally (to do with notions of time – see **temporal**). The most everyday way of thinking about a boundary is perhaps in a spatial way. This conjures up an image of a wall or a fence or some similar form of object or obstacle. In the office, a cubicle or partition separating different parts of the floor space is a typical illustration of this. Linguistically, received pronunciation, that is talking with an educated or 'posh' accent may, for example, to some people make the speaker seem more important or more educated than other individuals and can form boundaries within **identities**. Temporally, cut-off dates and deadlines are a clear example of a time-related boundary. Overall, a consequence of boundaries is that they delineate and invoke a range of possible **meanings**, interpretations and understandings.

Wherever boundaries are drawn or apparent, issues of, for example, **agency**, **identity** and **power** are often involved. In other words, actions and behaviours of an individual, individuals or institution(s) give rise to boundaries and in so doing introduce a capacity to control and direct. Furthermore, it is important to acknowledge that the introduction or existence of boundaries is just as likely to reproduce the establishment or emergence of yet further boundaries. **Critical Management Studies** (CMS) is very sensitive to the manners in which boundaries are perceived to exist and the effects that are produced and reproduced as a consequence of them (see **reproduction**). In particular, CMS accounts frequently charge **normative** and **managerialist** structures and practices with invoking reductionist and **representationalist** boundaries in a manner that is myopic, insensitive and even coercive and manipulative.

Key Words:

> Agency, Critical Management Studies, Discourse, Identity, Language, Meaning, Other, Power, Reductionism, Representationalism, Spatial, Temporal.

References

> Fleming and Spicer (2004); Gabriel and Willman (2004); Heracleous (2004); Hernes (2004); Keenoy and Seijo (2010); Paulsen and Hernes (2003); Sturdy, Clark, Fincham and Handley (2009).

Bricolage

The expression *bricolage* (from the French verb *bricoler* – to knock up, tinker with, fiddle about with) means the bringing together of potted or a random collection of objects or ideas. It also conveys the meaning of something that has been done by an enthusiast or, to coin a phrase, 'amateur inventor' rather than an expert in a particular domain. In everyday French expression, it is also used as the shop sign to indicate a Do-it-yourself (DIY) retail outlet which it can be seen correlates with the notion of 'trying to put things together/having a go at it'.

A *bricoleur* is an agent (see **agency**) of *bricolage* and is in essence a DIY enthusiast. Pejoratively *bricoleur* can also indicate somebody who has a go at something and invariably makes a botch of it.

A range of academic disciplines and philosophy have adopted the term in recent years. Within **Critical Management Studies** (CMS) writing, the term *bricolage* tends to be employed to portray, for example, a phenomenon, objects, elements, events or sets of issues that are pulled together in a manner that is diverse, improvised, experimental and borrowed from a range of sources and places. It represents (see **representation**) the creation or development of an argument, model, concept and/or understanding from an idiosyncratic collection of things – whatever is in hand is brought into play. In this sense the outputs and consequences of any *bricolage* can be unpredictable and prone to change and interpretation. It can therefore be seen that the concept of *bricolage* sits and works well with a range of philosophical traditions, such as **postmodernism** and **poststructuralism**, that tend to **privilege subjectivity** and relativity (as opposed to **objectivity** and **normative rationality**) that are frequently brought to bear in critical analyses.

Key Words:

Meaning, Postmodernism, Poststructuralism, Representation, Subjectivity.

References

Deuze (2006); Gabriel (2002); O'Doherty (2008); Quack (2007); Wagner-Tsukamoto and Tadajewski (2006).

Bureaucracy

The phenomenon of bureaucracy has long been a studied feature of organizations. Bureaucracy is frequently seen as employing a hierarchical form (see **hierarchy**) and style of organizational **structure** wherein the highest level of authority emanates from the top and flows downwards through middle-ranking tiers and then subsequently to staff and functions fulfilling more minor roles. In some regards, bureaucracy can also be seen as an aspect of organizational structure that provides standardized and efficient procedures to which professionals (or bureaucrats) of the organization can adhere in an objective manner, following carefully detailed rules in order to achieve organizational tasks.

From a more negative point of view, bureaucracy is often perceived as multi-layered and complex. It is shown as being composed of structures that are typically slow-reacting, ponderous and prone to stifling swift action and outcomes. Bureaucracies may also be caricatured as lacking personal warmth, faceless and unemotional which can lead to issues of depersonalization and dehumanization for those people who work in these structures, and also those individuals external to the organization who have to deal with them. Equally, bureaucratic environments may seem insensitive, domineering or bullying which raises questions of ethics, **politics** and organizational justice. Within bureaucratic environments, 'managers' often take the form of quasi-bureaucrats. Bureaucrats are represented as wrapping tasks up in red-tape and being bound by convoluted processes and procedures. Within critical texts and commentaries, bureaucracy is frequently couched as problematic and a feature of the **normative**, **managerialist** organizations.

Max Weber's (1864–1920) writings are among the most commonly cited works on bureaucracy. His study at the turn of the last century of, the then, newly emerging bureaucratic organizational forms in German states is considered a key moment in the literature on bureaucracy. The critique it offered is still widely applied and discussed in relation to modern organizations. Weber viewed these nascent bureaucratic forms as supplanting traditional structures in government, monarchy and religious spheres. His analysis concentrated on issues of **power** and **authority** and, in particular, a rational–legal authority wherein members of bureaucracies adhere to the rules governing relations and procedures between different levels of the **hierarchy** of the organization. It also considered issues of beliefs and **meanings** in systems, the role of specialization, centralization, technical **rationality** and expertise. Although Weber was concerned at the rapid spread of the bureaucratic phenomenon, he acknowledged its potential for efficiency in completion of tasks. Subsequent commentators such as Michel Crozier (1964), through his study on bureaucracies in France, argued that in reality all bureaucracies contain favouritism, cultural and political prejudice to some degree (see **culture** and **politics**).

Bureaucrats are most stereotypically associated with public sector organizations, although not exclusively, as many industrial or large business enterprises may also be prone to bureaucracy. In contemporary large public sector organizations, such as a National Health Service, emergency and rescue services and the Civil Service, bureaucrats and bureaucracy remain almost inevitably an enduring feature (Parker, 2000). Nevertheless, there has also been an increasing trend to introduce private sector **managerialist** type practices. This has led to the coining of the term 'New Public Sector Management' which points at an uncomfortable amalgam of existing bureaucratic and newly introduced private sector approaches.

It is also important to reflect on more extreme limits and dangers of bureaucracy in relation to its use of rationality and the possibility of dysfunctional **bureaucracy**. While a bureaucratic organization prizes **rationality**, not all outcomes of this might be reasonable or desirable. On occasion, the unfettered pursuit of rationality may produce impersonal, insensitive and even harsh, severe, tragic and horrific outcomes. Bauman (1989) explored this in relation to the Nazi Holocaust. He suggested that the rise and progression of bureaucratic forms, noted by Weber and amplified in the **modernity** of the twentieth century, had the inevitable consequence that they would be applied to a terrible end. The rational organization of the Holocaust, involving many thousands of bureaucrats and workers, invoked the rationalization of the separation of bureaucratic acts or means from brutal ends. Individuals working within Nazi controlled bureaucracies were responsible for rounding up millions of people, processing papers, organizing transport and facilities in order to ultimately send victims to concentration and extermination camps. Because the bureaucrats could not see the actual results or consequences of their actions (i.e. the murder of millions of people) they were able to detach emotion and possible **resistance** and carry out their daily job (see Jones, Parker and Ten Bos, 2005; Grey, 2008). The German military *Einsatz Gruppen* teams assigned to conduct the actual face-to-face executions and murders were not able to do such a separation of means and ends. This caused the Nazi extermination programme unforeseen delays and problems as members of the Einsatz Gruppen began to show signs that even they, as the perpetrators, could not endure such close proximity to unending atrocity. It was this, combined with the scale of murder envisaged, that led to the development of more systematized, mechanized industrial-scale process of the Nazi 'Final Solution'. Such systems allowed a sense of distance to be introduced for the executioner and the victims to be rendered less human and 'othered' (see 'other').

Suffice to say that in the contemporary era of management fashions which has seen the introduction of many of the initiatives aimed at making organizations flexible and able to react rapidly – examples include 'lean organizations', 'downsizing', 'just in time (JIT) delivery systems', 'business process re-engineering (BPR)' and so on and so forth have all, to some greater or lesser extent, targeted bureaucracy. Whether cast in a positive or pejorative light, bureaucracy is far from finished and in some shape or form remains a factor of modern organizational life.

Key Words:

Authority, Bureaucrat, Dysfunctional Bureaucracy, Managerialism, Modernity, Politics, Power, Rationality, Resistance, Technical Rationality.

References

Bauman (1989); Casey (2004); Courpasson and Clegg (2006); Crozier (1964); Du Gay (2000a, 2000b, 2005); Grey (2008); Jones, Parker and Ten Bos (2005); Knights and Willmott (2000); Parker (2000); Weber (1947, 1958).

Cc

Capitalism

Capitalism is a process whereby large sums of funds or monies for investment, that is capital, are invested in an economic project. A key characteristic of capitalism is that capital can be transferred around an economy, or between economies, seeking optimum rates of return on that capital investment. While this may be beneficial for the returns and profits of capital owners, the desire to optimize return on capital may result in disinvestment from one physical or geographical location in order to invest in another. For example, in recent decades, global capital transfers have resulted in the closure of high-cost factories in European countries in order to set up production in relatively low-cost Chinese and South East Asian economies. While this creates work and opportunities in the target destinations, it is also likely to lead to loss of jobs, livelihoods and careers, with all the related negative socio-economic effects, in the place from which capital investment is removed.

Capital can be publicly owned (i.e. government funding, stocks and loans) or privately owned (through private corporations listing shares on the stock-market and private companies where shares are not listed and are held by a small group of private individuals). However, more often than not references to capital and capitalism refer to private capital working within free-market (supply–demand) mechanisms. In making these investments capital owners usually own or command the required means of production which, in classical economic terms, encompasses *land* (including all industrial plant, factories), *labour* (the workforce, employees) as well as *capital*.

Capitalism has developed into a highly complex and sophisticated global market system. Equally, in theoretical terms, this practice is underpinned by a rich and diverse history and literature. Historically, writers such as Max Weber and Karl Marx produced seminal commentaries on capital and capitalism. Weber linked the Protestant work ethic to capitalist activity and was concerned about the new forms of **bureaucracy** that were coming into being as a result of industrialization. Marx was keen to point at the idea of asymmetrical, or uneven, **power** relations between powerful capitalists and other parties such as workers. Within these relations he underscored the notion of private **appropriation** of goods and capital (or ownership and possession) as contrasted with a socialized production (non-possession) wherein the means of production would be owned by the workers.

Marx also elaborated the idea of exploitation of labour (or workers) in the way that capitalists extracted *unshared added value* from workers. He saw this as a source of potential conflict. In the attempts and processes to maximize the extraction of labour value from the workforce and control potential conflict he observed processes that tended to centralize workers into factory-style locations and create a division of labour (the transformation of people moving from multi-activity, multi-tasking cottage-industry and craft ways of working to an organization where each person conducts a specialized, but often limited skilled task, repetitively). It was noted that such patterning of work provokes a range of forms of **alienation** among workers. A cumulative effect of such oppressive atmospheres is the creation of a sense of the shared conditions of class identity termed as *class consciousness* among the worker **proletariat**. This is turn may find **representation** and **resistance** in the form of organized labour through worker associations and trade unions. Marx considered that the capitalist class (which embodied to a great extent the Bourgeoisie – the affluent trading and merchant classes as opposed to historically landed aristocracy) would ultimately be usurped and displaced by the workers of the very system the Bourgeoisie had created and overseen. Subsequent contemporary comment and analysis have indicated that in the transformed work settings of the twentieth and twenty-first centuries, managerial and worker cooperation rather than conflict may, in some ways, be more prevalent and complex than supposed by Marx's theory at the time of his observations.

In contemporary times, capitalism has frequently been employed as a pejorative term to **represent** greedy super-rich individuals exploiting others. Typically illustrative of these concerns would be the very high levels of bonuses in the banking sector and chief executive pay and retirement packages frequently reported in the press. Indeed, some writers have argued that a capitalist system should concern itself only with the creation of wealth and surplus rather than social considerations. In other words, capitalism should focus solely with achieving the highest rate of return on capital. The wealth thus created would then 'trickle' down through society and, in theory, everyone would benefit from successful capitalists and entrepreneurs. To dedicate any time or energy to anything else should be seen as a misdirection of resource. Most prominently, this view has been advocated by Friedman (1970). In popular culture, it has been portrayed through characters such as the speculator Gordon Gekko in the Hollywood film *Wall Street* (1987) when in a speech to investors he proclaimed – 'Greed is good!' Nevertheless, in contrast to these notions, in recent years there has been an increasing debate concerning to what extent capitalistic systems should embrace social dimensions such as altruism, philanthropy, green, ethical, environmental and sustainability issues.

Marx recognized that capitalism would pass through periods of accumulation and collapse. Capitalistic systems would experience crises of confidence, reach a tipping point and be near implosion, or at the very least be partially diminished and dissembled, because normal transactions would seize up or cease. Major examples of this can be found in the Great Crash which started on Wall Street in 1926 and the more recent ongoing global banking and financial crisis in 2008–2009. Given these implications and consequences, this broaches the ethical and governance question concerning to what extent capitalist systems should be allowed to operate unchecked and/or unregulated. This is a concern that has become all the more prescient given near global financial meltdown in the beginning of the twenty-first century.

Although a number of economic systems have sought to employ alternative forms of economy to capitalist systems, for example, Soviet Communist central planning in the twentieth century, capitalism has still, by and large, become the dominant global system. Capitalism has now given rise to, and fused with, the phenomenon of globalization. Globalization has a number of facets including: the advent of emerging economies in Asia and South East Asia where the factors of production are cheap; the growth of flexible high volume capital and financial markets combined with the introduction of the Internet; the presence of mitigated trade protectionism among national economies; the dominance of pan-national trading blocs; and a social and political have all become centrally important in recent decades (see **politics**). Capital, capitalism and its associated market mechanisms are an integral aspect of the globalized experience and the phenomena of consumerism and **commodification** have become significant elements thereof.

Within markets in the Western hemisphere, service-based economies of post-industrial systems have become increasingly evident and it has become common to talk about less tangible forms of capital such as *human capital*. Human capital encompasses notions of intellectual, emotional and also social capital. Intellectual capital might include, for example, patents, innovation processes, software, brands and trademarks. Awareness by organizations of these aspects has given rise to development and employment of knowledge management as a competitive approach. Alternatively, emotional and social capital point at the social 'glue' that facilitates cohesion and satisfaction in the workplace and society at large (Bourdieu 1984; Coleman, 1988). For management this might be seen as something important in terms of harmonious team-working and productivity.

In relation to **Critical Management Studies** (CMS), it is important to make a number of connections with the ideas outlined above. **Labour Process Theory** (LPT) played a significant role in relation to aspects of the formative stages of CMS. Early LPT debates were intensely concerned with engagement with Marxist and left-wing political and sociological theory in attempts to analyse the conditions and **resistance** of workers challenging managerial attempts to control and shape work (see **Marxism, manager, managerialism** and **politics**). Braverman (1974), who examined employment environments and behaviours produced by capitalism, was an important and catalytic writer for the work of the LPT movement. This gave rise to the notion of *managerial capitalism* whereby managers gradually supplant the capital owners as directly steering and controlling the use and employment of capital.

As an area, CMS, although it has since taken different developmental trajectories to LPT, has nevertheless developed in relation to it (see Fournier and Grey, 2000). Work within CMS has brought, for example, **postmodern** and **poststructuralist** commentaries to bear on **Marxist** theoretical approaches. Given, the blurring of division of labour in the modern company setting, latterly CMS work has sought to critique the categorical delineation of work populations into managerial and worker groups or classes. As well as the traditional characterization of capitalist/manager versus labour/employee *inter-group* (between different groups) conflict, CMS has equally aimed to point up and analyse the *intra-group* struggles that may take place (between members within given groups) and the multitudinous issues of **power, resistance, discourse, voice** and **identity** that play out therein. It can be suggested that managers and non-managerial employees alike have a stake in making the prevailing system of capitalism work in order to extract their daily needs and a range of longer-term ambitions from the system. Of course, challenges to this position exist in a wide range of anti-capitalist lobby-groups and movements; however, it is certain that to attempt to replace capitalism would be likely to lead to major upheaval and disruption in any given transition period. In spite of the often very stark consequences of prevailing capitalist systems, and the potent potential of CMS to offer insights, the all too frequent response of CMS through, for example, postmodern and poststructuralist critiques has often been partial and ambivalent (on this issue see Linstead, 2004: 1–6).

Key Words:

> Alienation, Appropriation, Capital, Class Consciousness, Discourse, Exploitation, Human Capital, Identity, Intellectual Capital, Labour Process Theory, Post-Industrial, Post-Capitalist, Power, Private Appropriation, Proletariat, Resistance.

References

> Bell and Taylor (2003); Bourdieu (1984); Braverman (1974); Coleman (1988); Fournier and Grey (2000); Friedman (1970); Halsall (2008); Korczynski (2005); Marx (1867/1967); Weber (1947).

Cold War

The Cold War described the period of relations between the East (i.e. the Soviet Union) and West (essentially The United States of America and the North Atlantic Treaty Organization (NATO) countries which included the United Kingdom) political blocs in the post-Second World War period (see **politics**). This situation perpetuated between 1945 and 1989 until the fall of the Berlin Wall. It is impossible to separate the evolution of a wide array of social and economic spheres, such as management development, from major influences like the Cold War (Grey, 2008). Through the industrial military complex, management and organizations were effectively and variously on the 'home-front' of a propaganda war or the 'front-line' of an armaments and defence industry. The **capitalist** market system was seen as being in direct confrontation with the central planning of the communist Soviet regime (Linstead, Fulop and Lilley, 2009: 498).

The Cold War dichotomized the world into convenient and simplistic halves. In so doing it created an **'other'** which could be hated and feared (Kelley, Mills and Cooke, 2006: 603). It was a totally invasive phenomenon in that it pervaded and infiltrated relations in the arts, **politics**, commerce and wider social, cultural and economic dimensions (see **culture**). An illustration of this was the famous world championship chess match that took place in Reykjavik, Iceland, in 1972 between the American Bobby Fischer and Russian, Boris Spassky, the residing world champion. Fischer won the overall competition and it was billed as the cold war on the chess board by the media. In spite of the replete and expansive effect of the Cold War, Cooke (1999) has underlined that it has all but been written out of organization and management theory.

Clark (2000: 92) characterizes the period of the Cold War as one of modernization and romantic liberalism and shows how it involved the development of anti-**Marxist** theory. Much of early systems thinking embraced this spirit and purported to be politically neutral while in fact it was partisan to what Clark terms a 'an ideal variant of the North American civilisation' (ibid.). This was reported as consisting of 'tightly connected systems', linear trajectories (see **linearity**) from traditional to modern societies, and, involving incremental rather than **radical** (sic: revolutionary) change.

Key Words:

Berlin Wall, Capitalist, Industrial-Military Complex, Linearity, Politics, Radical.

References

Clark (2000); Cooke (1999); Fulop and Lilley (2009); Grey (2008, 2009); Kelley, Mills and Cooke (2006); Linstead (2004); Linstead, Fulop and Lilley (2009); Munro (2010).

Commodification (commodity)

A commodity is something that is produced or exists for which there is an identified demand. Commodification refers to the process(es) which result in someone or something being commodified and turned into a commodity. Frequently, a commodity is a product, good or entity which has gone through some process of 'production' and then, most importantly, it can be traded or function as a negotiable instrument in barter. In essence, it has been provided with an **identity** that involves economic value.

Within a Marxist (see **Marxism** and **capitalism**) understanding of commodification, the term is employed when an economic value is given to something which normatively would not necessarily carry an economic value such as, for example, **culture** or higher education (Willmott,

1995; Letiche, 2006). An illustration of this might include the manner in which we view certain parts of the countryside such as national parks or places of beauty. As such, they slowly become commodified through tourism which confers and develops a particular **identity** on popular places. In effect, the scenery, or the commodity becomes consumed – in this way there exists consumption of a particular resource. Here also, some stark examples can be conjured up, for instance, trafficking and ensnaring individuals into prostitution. Historically, the slave trade that contributed to building the early industrial wealth of Britain is a clear example of the commodification of human beings.

Key Words:

Commodity, Consumption, Product.

References

Dey and Steyaert (2007); Du Gay (1995); House (2001); Letiche (2006), Willmott (1995).

Conformity

Everyday organizational lives are replete with social norms, rules, **rituals** and guidelines which people are expected to observe and adhere to. When they follow these strictures, individuals are seen to fit in with, or conform, to the requirements of the organizational setting or context. Examples of conformity include, for example, when a person acts, speaks, dresses or engages in humour and so on and so forth in a similar way to those people around him or her. Conformity is often seen as important to group cohesiveness. However, when conformity becomes unquestioning there is a great danger that groupthink may be a consequence. In groupthink, the predominant pattern of questioning, conceptualizing and thinking goes in one direction only and ignores alternative ways of seeing issues and identifying solutions.

To not conform to what other people are following or doing can be viewed as highly problematic and even deviant. To do so, the individual risks being 'shut out' and not included in group(s). In this way, to not conform is to be treated as an **'other'**. The pressure to conform can therefore be very powerful and the decision to exercise independent judgement that runs counter to a wider group or community can be a difficult one for the person concerned. Not all non-conformity is seen as problematic. Some lack of conformity may act as a release for the other members of the group (Gabriel, Fineman and Sims, 2009).

Key Words:

Judgement, Other, Rituals, Rules, Social Norms.

References

Fineman, Sims and Gabriel (2009); Hodgson (2005); McKinlay (2002); Ten Bos (2005).

Consumption

Consumption stems from the verb 'to consume' which in its literal sense means to eat or drink. However, in its applied sense the act of consuming and the phenomenon of consumption have come to mean the using up, acquisition and even destruction of a given object or resource. Consumers are the people who undertake consumption.

With the growth of the role of the market, international trade and the impacts of globalization, consumption of a wide range of products, services and ideas has become readily accessible and available. This era grew out of the Industrial Revolution and expansion of late nineteenth and twentieth centuries which witnessed the birth and rise of mass production and mass consumption.

The growth of extensive consumption across a wide span of domains, not just in relation to goods and services but also in relations to issues of **identity**, **voice**, **power**, expression and so on and so forth, has led to a commensurate expansion of literature. It is commonplace for a range of disciplines to analyse the notions and implications of consumption and consumer behaviour (Du Gay, 1995; Miller, 2001).

Key Words:

Consumer, Identity, Power, Voice.

References

Du Gay (1995); Korczynski (2005); Miller (2001); Nayak and Beckett (2008); Sköld (2010).

Contingency

Contingency refers to a state of affairs in which something might or might not happen according to certain internal or external conditions. In this way, contingency is often contrasted with necessity. Something necessary must happen, while something contingent does not have to happen. So, for example, while it is necessary that the sun rise any given morning, it is a contingent matter whether or not a given person eats breakfast. Breakfast is contingent in the sense that it is not necessary (the person might sleep in) and it depends on other conditions (how late the individual stayed up and so on and so forth).

Management is as much about contingency as it is about necessity. When planning for the future, the concern is almost always to plan for contingencies. The manager asks: What might happen under certain conditions? If I want to build a bridge, it will pay to take into account what conditions I might come into contact with. It would be foolish to start building without checking the state of the ground underneath, how many people are likely to want to use the bridge, and what the likely future flow of the river will be. All of these matters of planning, which are obviously an important part of management, are matters of dealing with contingency. It is by no accident that managers plan in their budgets to try to keep some funds aside to cover 'contingencies'. They have 'contingency funds' in case things don't go as planned, and they purchase insurance policies against all manner of risk in case they haven't been careful enough to plan for other contingencies.

Once again, however, we can see that management involves some rather puzzling metaphysical problems together with ethical and political concerns (see **ethics** and **politics**). Dealing with contingency, and the activity of management as planning, involves considering the future. Moreover, most of the time when management is dealing with contingency, it is viewed as a problem rather than a natural or normal element. It is a problem that must be tamed, controlled, planned for and, in essence, managed. This issue points to some important things about the way that management deals with the future. Management seems to be concerned with the unpredictability that the future might bring. The future is filled with contingency, chance and risk, all of which involve the prospect that things might not go according to plan. This body of concerns has lead to the emergence and prominence of the area of 'risk management' in recent years.

It is often said that capitalism is a kind of economy in which certain people make investments and these investments are risky, in that they might not bring a return. Profit is the reward for taking risk. However, at the same time, a good part of what managers do is try to *avoid* risk (by planning for every possible contingency), and what financial planners do is to *avoid* making risky investments. After all, it would seem silly to speculate wildly when you could speculate with all of the information at your fingertips. This is one of the contradictions in the way that people often think about the need and rationale for management and markets.

Just like the operations of states and nations, organization involves a great deal of planning and gathering of information, and as little taking of risks as possible.

There is, however, another and perhaps more profound sense in which contingency is a *critical* concept for understanding management and organization. Here we are referring to the contingency of the very idea of management and markets. The question, to put it bluntly, is whether or not there is anything necessary about management and capitalism at all. Is management an essential, or a contingent thing, something that we will have for a while, but might one day pass?

Peter Drucker, a key commentator in management theory, wrote:

> The emergence of management as an essential, a distinct and a leading institution is a pivotal event in social history. Rarely, if ever, has a new basic institution, a new leading group, emerged as fast as has management since the turn of this century. Rarely in human history has a new institution proven indispensable so quickly; and even less often has a new institution arrived with so little opposition, so little disturbance, so little controversy. Management will remain a basic and dominant institution as long as Western civilization itself survives.
>
> (Drucker, 1954: 3)

There is a lot that could be said about Drucker's rather fantastic portrayal of the emergence of management, which by leaving out conflict and **resistance** to management remains at the very least historically false. But what is important in relation to the question of contingency is the way that Drucker makes the case for the necessity of management, by portraying management as something that is likely to be always present. Drucker's claims might be better understood by realizing that he was writing this at a high point in the **Cold War**, a time in which opinion was divided about American managerial capitalism. Drucker put management on the side of 'Western civilization', presuming that no one would ever speak ill of it.

In the twenty-first century we can still see arguments or claims of the kind that Drucker made during his long career. These appear in the common sense of what is variously called neo-liberalism, market **managerialism** or corporate **capitalism**, which tend to claim that management and capitalism are either completely unavoidable, or that they mark the highest form of civilization. As Margaret Thatcher once put it, not only is capitalism good, 'There is no alternative'. This effort to present managerial capitalism as universal and as necessary has been roundly criticized by a range of critics (see Parker, 2002a, 2002b; Böhm, 2006).

Butler, Laclau and Žižek (2000) remark on the lack of imagination that characterizes both conservatives and radical academic critics. They point out how today it is quite easy to imagine the end of the world, which will come in some great catastrophe such as ecological collapse, the rise of sea levels, storms, floods and tsunamis. But they note that, even at this time at which it is easy to think the end of the world, it has become all but unthinkable to imagine anything more than minor changes in the social structure or economic systems. This, of course, is a problem, in part because it blurs contingency and necessity. It sees one particular way of organizing production as essential and the continuation of the planet as contingent. Contingency is a critical concept in so far as it can offer the possibility of reversing such priorities.

Key Words:

Capitalism, Cold War, Ethics, Managerialism, Politics, Resistance, Risk.

References

Adler (2005a, 2005b); Böhm (2006); Butler, Laclau and Žižek (2000); Drucker (1954); Martens (2006); Parker (2002a, 2002b).

Critical accounting

In its conventional mode, accounting has traditionally been understood as a highly structured and procedural discipline and practice. Accounting conceived in this manner has been built on a number of core concepts and principles. These include, for example, the application and privileging of objective measurement with regard to transactions and the context in which they are set (see **privilege** and **objectivity**).

However, traditional approaches to accounting produce a number of challenges and potential problems. Accounting is vital to the operation of a company, but this is set within a complex web of human interactions and organizational issues. Using traditional accounting approaches it may be difficult to **represent** or encapsulate these rich environments.

Critical accounting embraces and invokes the spirit and analyses of **Critical Management Studies** (CMS) in relation to the accounting arena and was active from the beginning of CMS critiques (see Sikka and Willmott, 1996). In particular, critical accounting is keen to point at the many subjective (see **subjectivity**) aspects that play out in the composition of accounting records and relationships. Some of these subjectivities may already be acknowledged in the way that, for example, standard accounting practice attempts to value numbers for items such as bad debts, brand names, intellectual property or complex financial instruments such as derivatives. Critical accounting has also raised the issue of accounting history as, for example, social memory, accounting in relation to gender and class, the sociology of accounting, crime, the 'silence' of auditors or professionalization of the accounting sphere (Sikka, Haslam, Kyriacou and Agrizzi, 2007; Sikka, 2009). It is often the case that issues of subjectivity and interpretation in relation to accounting are the terrain of potential confusion, illusion or even misrepresentation and fraudulent actions (Sikka and Hampton, 2005). Study of this area has generated a wide range of interest and a number of dedicated journals including *Critical Perspectives on Accounting* and the *International Journal of Critical Accounting*.

Key Words:

Accounting Sociology, Interpretation, Representation, Subjectivity.

References

Sikka (2009); Sikka and Hampton (2005); Sikka, Haslam, Kyriacou, Agrizzi (2007); Sikka and Willmott (2010); Tinker and Carter (2003).

Critical Management Studies (CMS)

Critical Management Studies or CMS came to prominence in the early 1990s, although the ideas and philosophies from which it draws many of its ideas can be traced to earlier schools of thought and writings. **Critical Theory**, in particular, played an influential role at the outset of critical approaches and Alvesson and Willmott (1992, 1996) were among the key commentators in these catalytic phases of CMS. Over the subsequent two decades, CMS has embraced a wide range of philosophical stances including, among others, existentialism, **postmodernism**, **poststructuralism**, **critical realism** and **deconstructionism**.

CMS challenges the **normative** and **mainstream representations** of the structures and assumptions of human experiences in relation to organizational and managerial contexts and environments. It aims to critique and point up shortcomings in mainstream portrayals of management. Alvesson and Willmott (1996: 34) state that it is vital to challenge 'technocratic' representations of management. Equally, it is important not to accept that management is discussed in a mechanistic, **positivistic**, cause–effect manner. People working in organizations should not simply be seen as 'human resource' or 'human capital' and in over-coming a range of taken-for-granted assumptions there is scope to talk about issues of, for example, **power**, **oppression**, **identity**, **voice** and **resistance**.

The eclectic CMS movement and its adherents have always been self-conscious of the character, identity and direction of the field(s). Challenges to CMS and its legitimacy have also been an issue and Fournier and Grey (2000) initiated a significant discussion on these themes (see also Parker, 1995; Spicer, Alvesson and Kärreman, 2009 and Wisser, 2010). As CMS has developed it has, perhaps inevitably, become more institutionalized with the emergence of CMS-infused conferences such as the *Standing Conference on Organizational Symbolism* (SCOS); *European Group on Organizational Studies* (EGOS) and the bi-annual *International Critical Management Studies Conference* (CMS). Equally, some management departments are predominantly CMS-informed and a substantial number of professorial chairs are occupied by CMS academics. Moreover, a host of well-established CMS-influenced journals and publications also exist (see by way of illustration only, *Organization, Organization Studies, Culture and Organization, Ephemera*).

Key Words:

Critical Realism, Deconstructionism, Identity, Normative, Oppression, Positivism, Postmodernism, Poststructuralism, Power, Representation, Resistance, Voice.

References

Alvesson and Willmott (1992, 1996); Fournier and Grey (2000); Hotho and Pollard (2007); Parker (1995); Spicer, Alvesson and Kärreman (2009); Wisser (2010) – *see also the discussion in the 'Introduction' to this book and the further contemporaneous references made therein.*

Critical marketing

In some regards there is a parallel between critical marketing and **critical accounting.** Both discipline domains of **mainstream** marketing and accounting evolved and to some extent continue as highly **normative** areas. This was especially the case in the early decades of the twentieth century where there were few critical insights and inputs. Marketing was frequently characterized as the hand-in-hand ally of a capitalist market system (Packard, 1960; Marcuse, 1991).

Nevertheless, a sense of criticality emerged in relation to marketing as early as the 1970s and a number of **mainstream** commentators began to embrace a need to develop the scope of the discipline in order to take account of alternative organizational forms rather than just traditional corporate ones (Kotler and Levy, 1969; Kotler, 1972). Marketing has undergone a critical infusion and growth in recent decades in parallel with the general emergence of **Critical Management Studies** (CMS). This movement has seen an ongoing attempt for marketing to acknowledge and take account of 'radical social, economic and political change' (Burton, 2001) embracing perspectives pertaining to **commodification**, consumption, **ethics**, historical and political perspectives (see, for example, Tadajewski and Jones, 2008a, 2008b, 2008c; Tadajewski, 2009b) (see **politics**).

Key Words:

Commodification, Critical Management Studies, Mainstream, Normative, Politics.

References

Burton (2001); Kotler (1972); Kotler and Levy (1969); Marcuse (1991); Packard (1960); Tadajewski (2009b); Tadajewski and Jones (2008a, 2008b, 2008c).

Critical Realism

Critical Realism is a philosophical approach that builds on the assumption that what people broadly and *prima facie* (i.e. 'at first sight') sense with many of their primary senses (facts regarding, for example, number, height or movement of things) is accurate and true. In other words this provides some form of **objectivity** in relation to external objects that surround us. This contrasts with more relativistic approaches which may challenge the very existence of such objects. However, through Critical Realism, the manner in which secondary qualities (for example, sight, taste, smell) create sensations in individuals in relation to these objects may vary considerably and this is a *subjective* dimension (see **subjectivity**). In this way, Critical Realism places greater emphasis on 'what is' and its reality, that is **ontology**, and the way it shapes our perceptions rather than approaches such as, for example, **postmodernism** and **poststructuralism**.

In terms of positioning Critical Realism in relation to other philosophies, it can be seen that its blend of the objective and subjective places it somewhere between the commitments of an approach like positivism (which prizes **objectivity**) and **postmodernism** or **poststructuralism** (which **privilege** more relativistic subjective approaches).

Critical Realism is inextricably associated with the writings of Bhaskar (1989) but has been addressed and developed in organization and management studies by a range of commentators (see Ackroyd and Fleetwood, 2001; Contu and Willmott, 2005; Fleetwood and Ackroyd, 2004; Fleetwood, 2005; Fairclough, 2005; Reed, 2005; Willmott, 2005).

Key Words:

Meaning, Objectivity, Ontology, Positivism, Postmodernism, Poststructuralism, Subjectivity.

References

Ackroyd and Fleetwood (2001); Bhaskar (1989); Contu and Willmott (2005); Fairclough (2005); Fleetwood (2005); Fleetwood and Ackroyd (2004); Mutch (2005); Reed (2005); Willmott (2005).

Critical Theory

Critical Theory is a school of thought and set of philosophical ideas. It emerged from, and is associated with, what is termed The Frankfurt School which was based around the Institute of Social Research in Frankfurt primarily during the 1920s and 1930s but also in the post-war period. Among the key commentators associated with the School are Herbert Marcuse (1898–1979), Max Horkheimer (1895–1973), Theodor Adorno (1903–1969), Eric Fromm (1900–1980) and more latterly Jurgen Habermas (1929–). The writings of its key commentators have exerted a very powerful influence over critical perspective approaches. This influence was particularly evident in some of the early and groundbreaking books that instigated the wider development of CMS (see Alvesson and Willmott, 1992, 1996).

In broad terms, The Frankfurt School builds its work on the commentaries of Marx and Freud (see **Marxism**). Emerging from the **Enlightenment** in Western philosophy and experience, The Frankfurt School identified the **alienation** evident in society and sought ways in which society could develop knowledge and be emancipated (see **emancipation**) not just from commercial or contractual arrangements but also in terms of intellectual, moral, artistic and **aesthetic** ideas. Critical Theory is a theory which wrestles with the challenge of how to change society as a whole.

While Critical Theory has been an important, even central, aspect of the development of many approaches and much work in CMS, it would be incorrect to suggest that it is the key or unique influence. CMS embraces a broad spectrum of other philosophical approaches including *inter alia* **postmodernism**, **poststructuralism**, **deconstructionism** and **Labour Process Theory** all of which have been employed in critical texts and analyses.

Key Words:

>   Aesthetics, Alienation, Deconstructionism, Emancipation, Frankfurt School, Labour Process Theory, Marxism, Postmodernism, Poststructuralism.

References

>   Alvesson and Willmott (1992, 1996); Fleetwood (2005); Malpas and Wake (2006); Sim and Van Loon (2005); Willmott (2005).

Culture

'Culture' is a term covering, and referring to, a vast sphere of influences and commentaries. Culture concerns art, issues of taste and judgement, together with intellectual, artistic and social development. To employ the term 'cultured' in connection with a person or group is a positively loaded term meaning that he, she or they exhibit educational, artistic and intellectual qualities and taste.

In relation to organization and management, culture is commonly associated with the term *corporate culture* which means the values, beliefs, atmospheres, customs and practices, goals and missions that are found in an organization. Each and every organization will have nuances and differences in the patterns of its own corporate culture.

In **mainstream** and **normative** writings, corporate culture is discussed as something that managers need to understand, build, shape and manage so that it can assist in the achievement of higher production, effectiveness and **performativity**. From this perspective, attempts by individuals or groups to go against the culture or to not 'fit in' are seen as **resistance**.

Critical accounts take issue with **normative** texts that tend to view culture as a fixed and well-defined entity with clearly defined boundaries that can be shaped and controlled by managers (see **boundary**). Critical perspectives are likely to question whether it is possible at all to talk about the existence of coherent, fixed, structured and stable culture in an organization. From a critical take on cultures in organizations, it is more common to talk about culture being constituted of organic and evolving patterns of behaviour, shifting **power** alliances and emergent **discourses**, **narratives** and **identities** rather than being fixed in nature.

Key Words:

Beliefs, Discourses, Identity, Mainstream, Narratives, Normative, Performativity, Power, Resistance, Values.

References

Alvesson (2002); Badham, Garrety, Morrigan and Zanko (2003); Parker (2000); Rhodes and Parker (2008); Sköld (2009).

Cybernetics

Cybernetics involves the study of the interactions that occur within control and communication systems. Therein, the idea of communication systems spans a range of possibilities including human exchanges, automatic or intelligent machine mechanisms or even living organisms. Systems and mechanisms and their cybernetic networks and interactions have long been part of human work and life experience. A central aspect of a cyber system is that one action or exchange between one part of the system (or between one person located in the system) and another part (or person) in the system is likely to lead to impacts and consequences further on in the mechanisms or networks. These consequences may be linear (see **linearity**) in character but also may return via other connections and interactions to the original message transmitter. Thus, they display cyclical and feedback characteristics. Indeed, one action may indeed cause a wide range of actions and reactions in a rhizomatic manner (see **rhizome**).

Mechanisms and systems have been an important and prevalent part of human life for millennia and the above issues have been an integral aspect of these. In the contemporary era, information technology has introduced novel cybernetic experiences and dimensions. In particular, the speed, scope, power and possibilities of the Internet have produced radical cybernetic information proliferation and exchange (Armitage and Roberts, 2002).

Key Words:

Communication, Feedback, Internet, Rhizome, System.

References

Amalya and Montgomery (2001); Armitage and Roberts (2002); Cooper (2010); Grey (2009); Munro (2010).

Dd

Deconstructionism

Deconstructionism is a philosophical body of thought concerned with exploring **language** in texts and the way in which the interplay of words in texts create and provide meaning in relation to a given subject. This particular view of **discourse**, or discursive philosophy of deconstructionism, is closely associated with the French philosopher Jacques Derrida and is often associated with the field of **postmodernism** but more frequently **poststructuralism**.

Deconstructionism offers a very different perspective to what Derrida saw in many prevailing approaches to building **meaning** and **knowledge** (Derrida, 1976). Derrida believed that extant approaches often sought to find the essence or **truth** located at the heart of matter or topic. Derrida contested the ultimate possibility of this, suggesting that words are not in fact 'fixed' in their meaning (as they are often, by way of illustration, presented in a dictionary) rather they glean their meaning from their mutual interaction in a given text or context.

Deconstructionism has been widely employed in various guises within **Critical Management Studies** (CMS) critiques (see Cooper, 1989; Chia, 1996; Jones, 2007, 2010). Deconstructionism challenges the **normative** face value of words and terms. It exposes what expression seeks to embrace and, equally, what it, deliberately or inadvertently, ignores or **silences**. In other words, texts are not necessarily or automatically viewed as neutral or innocent. They often contain assumptions and implied notions of what is good or bad, right, wrong or inappropriate.

Jones (2004) provides an interesting and valuable overview of Derrida's life and work and investigates the ways in which deconstructionism has variously been addressed or invoked as a method. He notes that on occasion, use of deconstructionism by some commentators has been prone to be in a negative, rather than affirmative or relativistic posture and this is rooted in particular periods, **politics** and **ethics** (especially with regard to **Marxism**).

Key Words:

Discourse, Meaning, Postmodernism, Poststructuralism, Silence.

References

Allard-Poesi (2005); Chia (1996); Cooper (1989); Derrida (1976); Jones (2004, 2007, 2010); Thanem (2006).

Deductivism (adjective: deductive)

Deductivism is an approach to research which operates on the basis of constructing a **hypothesis** or **hypotheses** for which data are subsequently collected that can be tested in order to prove or disprove the validity of a given **hypothesis**. By developing a range of individual hypotheses, it tends to move from a general conceptual framework to a particular focal point or particular truth. This form of approach is often associated with a belief system that prizes notions of logic and **rationality**. In this regard, it is commonly associated with a positivistic approach to research (see **positivism**). Deductivism is not a widely used approach in **Critical Management Studies** (CMS) which alternatively tends to value more inductive, interpretive and ethnographic approaches.

Key Words:

Hypothesis, Positivism, Rationality.

References

Bryman and Bell (2007); Clegg, Kornberger and Pitsis (2008).

Determinism

Determinism is a philosophical and methodological belief and approach that argues it is possible to identify particular factors (or variables) that cause certain effects. As a scientific concept, centrally positioned in experimental technique it values **objectivity** and **rationalism**. This means that determinism believes that it does not see or value a role for human interpretation or subjective context in the creation of cause and effect (see **subjectivity**).

Within organization and management an illustration of this issue is pointed up in relation to technology. Some commentators would argue that the introduction of a given technology inevitably and unavoidably causes a series of effects independent of human interaction with it, that is, the introduction of a new computer system seemingly (and for determinists, almost expectedly and automatically) changes human behaviour and brings about efficiencies. This perspective is termed *technological* **determinism**. Differing commentators, including for example those coming from a critical perspective stance, would suggest that human interaction with, and in relation to, the technology *creates* and **socially constructs meaning** and effects of that technology and would view technological determinism as an oversimplified cause–effect account (McLoughlin and Badham, 2005).

Key Words:

Meaning, Objectivity, Subjectivity, Technological Determinism.

References

Leca and Naccache (2006); McCabe (2010); McLoughlin and Badham (2005); Salaman and Storey (2008).

Deviance

'Deviance' is the term given to behaviour that is identified as being different to what might be considered as normal or **normative**. In what may be termed 'conventional management practice and theory' (see entries on **mainstream**, **normative**, **modernism** and **capitalism**) deviance by employees is not considered acceptable or tolerable. In **modernistic** settings, there is a *prima facie* assumption that the firm is operating as a **unitary** organization, that is, everyone adheres to a given or shared set of values, **culture** and mission. Where deviance or departure from these values is identified among employees it is often perceived or understood as **resistance** that must be stopped or overcome by management action. This might be through straightforward aggressive confrontation as in, for example, during heated industrial unrest or disputes, or alternatively and more insidiously, through day-to-day 'performance management'. This latter approach might involve the use of targeted training and development interventions or the use of disciplinary and monitoring procedures to check that the 'deviant' employee(s) is behaving in a more **normative** and performative manner (see **performativity**).

It can be seen that **Critical Management Studies** (CMS) approaches are likely to show a great interest in the concept and experience of deviance and the various forms it might take. A central commitment of CMS is the exploration of ways in which **normative** or **mainstream** approaches might be challenged or found wanting. Exploring acts of deviance in the workplace is an important aspect of such investigations. Deviance might be construed as an attempt to seek some form of **emancipation** from the controls and constraints in the workplace. Alternatively, it might be motivated by a desire to impede a new development of, or change being introduced into, the workplace. It may simply be for amusement, fun and to relieve boredom in monotonous or tiresome work situations (Ackroyd and Thompson, 1999). Deviance may often not be apparent or visible and Gabriel (2005) has discussed the notion of 'unmanageable' spaces in employee thoughts that are beyond the reach of organizational or managerial control. This theme is also recurrent in literature beyond organization and management. Famously, George Orwell's well-known 1948/49 novel *Nineteen Eighty-Four* portrays a much changed, dark and futuristic United Kingdom. The novel's protagonist Winston deviates from, and battles against, the ruling totalitarian party edicts variously using his mind and body in a range of, ultimately disastrous, acts of resistance.

Key Words:

Control, Emancipation, Mainstream, Normative, Resistance, Unitary.

References

Ackroyd and Thompson (1999); Badham, Garrety, Morrigan and Zanko (2003); Gabriel (2005); Orwell (1948/49); Zhang, Spicer and Hancock (2008).

Dialectics

The term 'dialectics' stems from philosophical **discourse** and refers to a method of logic that aims to identify **truth** by contrasting and testing two sets of opposing ideas. In the interaction between the two sets of ideas one variously shapes the other in a series of mutual pushes and pulls that creates a dialectic between them. Commonly, the term 'dialectic' has been associated with Marxist theory and commentary and underlines the tension between various groupings and agents in **capitalist** systems (typically proletariat workers, capitalists, bourgeois and land owning aristocratic classes and **power** factions) (see **Marxism** and **capitalism**).

In the contemporary workplace it is possible to identify a range of possible dialectics that might play out between different groups of employees, for example, between non-managerial employees and **managers**, between different sections and team of workers, between various divisions of an organization, between elite groupings or between Trades Unions and company representatives and so on and so forth. It is important not to suggest that dialectic implies only conflict. Even collaboration may involve dialectical aspects and dimensions (Clegg, Kornberger and Pitsis, 2008).

It may also be possible to consider the existence of internalized dialectics played out within a given individual whereby a dilemma or tension of, for instance, various aspects of **identity** may be in dialectical opposition and contest – that is how does a person sense they are behaving as opposed to how they would like to behave and be.

Key Words:

Capitalism, Discourse, Identity, Marxism, Power, Truth.

References

Clegg, Kornberger and Pitsis (2008); Hellström (2004); Mueller and Carter (2005); Pina e Cunha (2004).

Discipline (also disciplinary)

Discipline has long been a central theme of organization and management. In 1914, Fayol stated it as one of the 14 principles on which management and organization should operate. In this he understood discipline to mean that workers should follow the orders and directions of managers but he also recognized the need for managers to be competent if orders were to be followed effectively and with conviction by workers (Fayol, 1914/1949).

Within **Critical Management Studies** (CMS), the work of Foucault (1979) has been extensively used and applied in relation to discipline. In particular, his text *Discipline and Punish: the Birth of the Prison* has been a key resource that organization studies, and especially critical approaches, have drawn upon. In this work, Foucault, among other things, provides an understanding that humanism and its focus on the individual (rather than a divine or supernatural figure) and human **sense-making** and **identity** has created the possibility of categorizing and organizing the individual and the world which he or she inhabits. This affords the individual opportunities for autonomy, **agency**, action and very importantly **power.** However, reciprocally, and perhaps less desirably, this also lends the individual to be controlled, himself or herself, by the very regimes (and power they exercise) to which he or she has been party in creating and sustaining (Knights, 2004: 24). Linstead argues that the *Discipline and Punish* strand of Foucault's work has been 'over-represented in organization studies' and really, rather than Foucault's work being applied to organization studies, it would perhaps be more beneficial and enlightening if organization studies were applied to Foucault (Linstead, 2004: 19).

Foucault's work shows that individuals are not necessarily simply controlled by disciplinary structures, **bureaucracies** and corporate **cultures** but actually may *internalize* aspects, particularly disciplinary ones, of these cultures so that they effectively auto-discipline. By this it is meant that individuals keep themselves under disciplinary control in the belief, for example, that **surveillance** is taking place on them all the time, whether it is in fact or not (also see **panopticon**). In effect, the very thought that we are being watched may cause us constantly to check and modify our behaviour. Therefore, in the long run, the power and disciplinary regime does not need to formally or visibly exert power because the members of the organization essentially self-regulate. It should be underlined that it is not just in relations between individuals that discipline might be discussed but also teams and teamwork have an important role in policing and sustaining disciplinary regimes.

Key Words:

Bureaucracy, Culture, Foucault, Identity, Punish, Sense-making, Surveillance.

References

Fayol (1949); Foucault (1979); Knights (2004); Linstead (2004); Winiecki (2009).

Discourse

Basic or preliminary understandings of discourse tend to indicate it as a conversation, an exchange or series of expressions. Within social sciences, more academic concepts relating to discourse have expanded it into a rich and varied field. Discourse is often (and perhaps over-simplistically) seen as something akin to **language**. However, it is inextricably connected to what has become termed 'the linguistic turn' in the social sciences, wherein, **language**, signs, **stories**, **narratives** and symbols (see **symbolism** and **semiotics**) among other things are seen as crucially important in creating **meaning** and **sense-making** in understanding situations and contexts. This contrasts sharply with earlier alternative views on language which tended to see discourse as neutral and merely a synonym for communicating. Foucault's work has been extensively referred to in critical commentaries particularly illustrating how discourse interweaves with **power**. Through our engagement with discourse we not only make, or produce, **meaning** and power relations but we equally **reproduce** them.

Processes of discourse analysis involve the use of approaches and techniques to dissect, investigate and understand what is taking place in given discourse(s) (Fairclough, 2010). Views on discourse and discourse analysis cover a broad span. Some commentators see discourse and discursive exchanges in organizations as *actually forming* or *making* the organization in effect. In other words, through their everyday myriad interactions people make organizations via discourse.

Alternatively, other writers are less comfortable with the idea that discourse plays such a significant role in creating, constituting and making sense and meaning in organizations. While they see a role for discourse in organizations, other 'facts' and 'events' have their own solidity, concreteness and ontological reality beyond the boundaries of discursive exchanges (see **ontology** and **boundary**). In this latter view, solid objects such as products, machines and buildings *exist* and the role of discourse is that people may develop subjective (see **subjectivity**) meanings and perspectives in relation to them. Thus, discourse is variously important in work rooted in, for example, **postmodern**, **poststructuralist** and **deconstructionist** philosophical approaches. This contrasts with, for example, **positivism**, which sees objects as external to the observer (waiting to be objectively (see **objectivity**) explored and discovered) and sees little or no role for discourse and subjectivity in these processes.

In critical writing it is common to refer to various large categories or types of discourse, for example, 'organizational discourse' or 'managerial discourse'. 'Managerial discourse' alludes to a discourse exhibiting managerialist (see **managerialism**) tendencies and traits. This kind of reference is employed as a type of shorthand for a generic area and the assumptions underpinning the prevalent discourses that take place within it. Another way of talking about the recurrent way a particular discourse occurs is to refer to it as a *discursive practice* (Grant, Hardy, Oswick and Putnam, 2004).

Key Words:

Language, Meaning, Narrative, Objectivity, Ontology, Positivism, Semiotics, Stories, Subjectivity.

References

Alvesson and Kärreman (2000); Bell and Taylor (2004); Fairclough (2010); Grant, Hardy, Oswick and Putnam (2004); Hardy (2004); Samra-Fredericks (2005); Whittle (2008).

Disneyization

The term 'Disneyization' refers to processes whereby organizations employ characteristics and practices exemplified by the famous Disney organization. At one level, Disney is world famous for its many fantasy characters and colourful stories aimed at embodying fantasies or dreams that children and adults can fulfil. Within the Disney company employees are known as 'cast members' and, in a similar manner to the retailer WalMart, employees are also referred to as 'associates'. **Discourses** such as these in organizations like Disney show the **power** of representing (see **representation**) people and things in a particular way and begin to illustrate the power of *Disneyfied* **discourses** and cultures.

Nevertheless, at other levels, commentators of organization and management have indicated a potentially less attractive side to processes of Disneyization and the organizations that employ them. Boje (1995) pointed at contradictions in official Disney rhetoric and publications. Van Maanen (1991) showed how a wide range of discontentment reigned among employees behind the scenes in Disney sites. This involved actions and resistance by 'cast members' (in other words: employees) against troublesome colleagues and customers. Various critiques have similarly signalled the downsides of **capitalism**, corporatism, **commodification**, consumption and consumerism that are concealed behind the *façade* of the spectacle, illusion and fantasy. Bryman (2004) in his work *The Disneyization of Society* discussed how many of the aspects of Disney processes are applied and operational in relation to a wide range of organizations and areas of society beyond the Disney Company. Much of this commentary parallels Ritzer's famous work on **McDonaldization** which identified and discussed how the practices and processes employed by McDonald's in its global activities are being rolled out in health care, education and governmental sectors.

Key Words:

> Commodification, Consumerism, Consumption, Discourses, *Façade*, McDonaldization, Power, Representation.

References

> Boje (1995); Bryman (2004); Gabriel (2005); Van Maanen (1991).

Diversity

Diversity underlines that people, objects or issues exhibit varying and differing characteristics. In this way, they are different or diverse. Within a contemporary management and organizational context, diversity is often raised as a part of equality and diversity policies in organizations. This involves ensuring that prejudice and bias do not occur in relation to, for example, race, sexual orientation, religion and beliefs. Such organizational policies have the goal of ensuring that a company or organization takes account of various laws and regulations and also an ethical spirit (see **ethics**) of the most constructive and appropriate behaviours that should take place.

In **normative** and **mainstream** commentaries on organizations, diversity is presented as something that everyone should be aware of and that mangers need to manage (see **managerialism**). This activity will usually be overseen and guided by the human resource management department. The frequent assumption is that, by managing diversity issues in the most effective and efficient manner, the performance of employees and the overall organization can be enhanced (see **performativity**).

The increased attention focused on diversity in recent times has given rise to the field of *Diversity Studies*. This sphere has attracted scholars from both **normative** and critical stances (see **Critical Management Studies**). Whereas **mainstream**, **normative** approaches focus on heightening **performativity** through effective diversity policies, in contrast, critical approaches are more likely to analyse issues of **power**, **voice** and **identity** and the ways these play out through diversity debates and issues in organizations. The existence of diversity policies and diversity studies does not of course mean that all issues of equality have been addressed. Illustrative of this is the relatively low representation of women and ethnic minorities in senior/director positions in a wide range of organizational settings (see Wajcman, 1998).

Key Words:

Equal Opportunity, Identity, Power, Voice.

References

Greene and Kirton (2009); Kirton and Greene (2009); Kirton and Greene (2010); Tomlinson and Schwabenland (2010); Wajcman (1998); Zanoni, Janssens, Benschop and Nkomo (2010).

Dualism

'Dualism' means twofold or composed of two entities and stems from the idea within philosophy that a given sphere or domain can be comprised primarily of two distinct variables. Scanning over historical philosophical debate it is easy to locate such dualities – mind and body, good and bad, form and content are three such examples.

In historical philosophical terms, dualism is closely associated with the French philosopher Rene Descartes (1596–1650), giving rise to the idea of *Cartesian dualism*. In particular, he proposed that the mind and the body were quite separate and explored the consequences of this. This is popularly evoked in his well-known expression 'I think, therefore I am.' Descartes' work has had a great influence on subsequent philosophical work. His legacy endures particularly in continental rationalistic (see **rationality**) thinking, especially in France. This is seen as very much contrasting with a historical British tradition of pragmatism and **empiricism.**

Dualism is seen as being closely associated with, and underpinning, positivistic, objectified and delineated ways of seeing the world (see **positivism**, **objectivity** and **linearity**). Therefore, dualism is closely aligned with managerialistic (see **managerialism**) approaches (Watson, 2006). Large swathes of **normative** and **mainstream** management and organizational commentary value ideas of objectivity. They largely detach notions of subjectivity, employing metrics for measuring and assessing organizational outputs. This underpins a pre-occupation of focussing on attempts to achieve heightened effectiveness and **performativity**. These are, of course, typical areas that form a basis of critique for **Critical Management Studies** (CMS). CMS critiques tend not to adopt or employ dualistic thinking as part of their approach. Dualism is seen as too fixated with categorically delineating the subjects it considers whereas CMS have a tendency to see boundaries as discursive, shifting or at best difficult and challenging to fix in any definitive or permanent manner (see **boundary** and **discourse**).

Key Words:

Boundary, Empiricism, Linearity, Objectivity, Positivism, Rationality.

References

Caldwell (2007); Watson (2006); Willmott (2005).

Ee

Emancipation

Emancipation is the act of setting free or ensuring liberty and freedom for people, organizations and environments. Emancipatory concepts and ideals have been a central concern and debate in philosophy for thousands of years. In particular, the **Enlightenment** period in the Western world (broadly spanning the seventeenth and eighteenth centuries) developed a wide range of ideas and debates in relation to freedoms. These informed, for example, the declaration of rights and acts of independence in transforming nations such as the new French Republic and newly forming nations such as the United States of America.

For organization and management, emancipation has remained an important and recurrent theme. Marxist philosophy (see **Marxism**, **Capitalism** and **Labour Process Theory**) with its goal of empowering (see **empowerment**) the proletariat has infused a considerable amount of commentary in relation to how this might be accomplished in work settings. Fournier and Grey (2000) illustrate how closure of sociology departments in the United Kingdom in the 1970s and 1980s and subsequent migration of left-wing-influenced academics to newly emerging business schools infused Marxist emancipatory ideals and thinking into the business and organization academic environment. This had significant catalytic implications in relation to the *naissance* of **Critical Management Studies** (CMS). In particular, Alvesson and Willmott in their 1992 and 1996 publications made early developments in CMS, drawing on **Critical Theory**. Like much of the writing that followed, this work sought to identify emancipatory outlets from oppressive organizational and managerial control and **power** as a key objective for critical perspectives. Often such emancipatory success may be small-scale or limited to a local context. In these instances it is common to refer to these as *micro-emancipations* (Spicer, Alvesson and Kärreman, 2009).

Key Words:

Capitalism, Critical Theory, Empowerment, Enlightenment, Freedom, Liberty, Marxism, Micro-Emancipation, Oppression, Power.

References

Alvesson and Willmott (1992, 1996); Atkin, Hassard and Cox (2007); Fournier and Grey (2000); Kavanagh (2009); Spicer, Alvesson and Kärreman (2009); Willmott (2005).

Emergence

Emergence concerns the idea of something evolving and developing gradually rather than exhibiting a fixed and unchanging nature. While emergence has not particularly developed as a widely adopted or clearly defined body of theoretical thought, the general concept of emergence has been an attractive one in critical approaches (see Watson and Harris, 1999).

Mainstream or **normative** bodies of management commentary have a tendency to talk about the idea of moving or changing from one fixed structure to another, for example, moving from one role to a new one, or, moving through the various stages of a strategic plan. In contrast, **Critical Management Studies** (CMS)-style commentaries are more likely to want to portray such developments as multi-faceted, gradual and evolutionary, indeed, emergent, rather than moving in a linear, predictive, mechanistic or staged manner (see **linearity**). Emergent changes are organic and to some greater or lesser extent unpredictable. In discussions on emergence it is not uncommon to refer to **social constructionism** as one way of explaining or discussing the processes whereby emergence takes place. Thereby, people through interaction and **sense-making** processes cause thinking, events and actions to evolve over the course of time.

Key Words:

Evolving, Mainstream, Normative, Sense-making, Social Constructionism.

References

Robertson and Swan (2004); Tsoukas (1998); Watson and Harris (1999).

Emotion

With the increasing influence of sociological and psychological approaches within organization and management contexts, emotion has come to be seen as playing an important role. Expression, suppression and oppression of emotion have a long-established tradition in areas of Western experience. Max Weber (1864–1920) pointed this up in his extensive discussions on **bureaucracy** and the Protestant work ethic. Equally, the privileging of rationalism in the **Enlightenment** did much to relegate emotion to something that would interfere with objective reasoning (see **privilege**, **rationality** and **objectivity**).

In **Critical Management Studies** (CMS), there has been a significant expansion of the discussion on emotion and the **subjective** dimensions to which it gives rise. Fineman's (1993, 2003) work on emotion added significant impetus to the debate and drew on a number of sources to illustrate how emotions are characterized, employed and also marginalized in work and organizational contexts. A significant influence in this discussion was the work of Arlie Hochschild *The Managed Heart: Commercialization of Human Feeling* published in 1983. Therein, she explored the notion of *emotional labour* and the ways in which emotional issues arise in people's work. In other words, people invest much more of themselves in their work roles than in the simple act of performing tasks. Customer service involving smiles, eye contact, and displays of sincerity, compassion, warmth and friendliness are all examples of this. In some arenas, such as work at Disney (see **Disneyization**) or other entertainment and service outlets behaving in this way is a stipulated condition of behaviour at work.

In early periods of the twentieth century, emotion was not considered a relevant factor to discuss as part of workplace. However, in the contemporary era, emotion has become very much part of **normative** and **mainstream** approaches to management. Illustrations of this include a growing literature on *emotional intelligence*, *neuro-linguistic programming* (NLP), *management coaching* and the acknowledgement of the role of emotion in a wide range of organizational areas, including for example, leadership, team and group work.

Nevertheless, CMS remains intensely concerned that **mainstream** engagement on emotion-related topics is essentially managerialist (see **managerialism**). In this regard, **normative** approaches are seen as engaging with issues of emotion only in so far as it can be controlled and employed to the ends of greater corporate effectiveness, efficiency, profitability and **performativity** rather than being primarily aimed at the benefit of the individual.

Key Words:

Disneyization, Managerialism, Objectivity, Rationalism, Subjective.

References

Callahan (2004); Fineman (1993, 2007); Gabriel (2005); Hochschild (1983); Korczynski (2003); Phillips and Rippin (2010).

Empiricism

Empiricism is a belief and a process in developing knowledge through observation and experimentation using the human senses. This is in contrast to, for example, developing a theory solely through abstract thought and reflection, that is to say, not necessarily grounded in experience or human senses. As a general stance, it is often suggested as a traditional value and approach to **sense-making** and developing **meaning** in Anglo-Saxon contexts (also see **Enlightenment** and **positivism**).

Key Words:

Anglo-Saxon, Human Senses, Meaning, Sense-making.

References

Bryman and Bell (2007); Collins (2004); Tadajewski (2009a); Whitley (2003).

Empowerment

'Empowerment' is a term which, in recent years, has become increasingly employed in organizational and managerial contexts. Empowerment is a process whereby **power** in making decisions and running parts of an organization's activities is granted by managers to employees who did not previously hold that power. This may have the effect of releasing managers or leaders, who previously held that role or task, to pursue other activities and, equally, it might make the employees who receive the power more fulfilled or satisfied at having more control over their job and actions.

Because the term 'empowerment' has occasionally been employed in a disingenuous or manipulative way in organizational contexts, the term has attracted a degree of ridicule and cynicism. For some commentators, empowerment can be seen as a new piece of jargon doing no more than replacing 'old-fashioned' managerial control (see **managerialism**) with soft approach that still transfers onerous responsibility, accountability and even culpability or blame onto the employees. For these reasons, critical approaches have shown a cautionary approach to empowerment. On the one hand, the **emancipatory** (see **emancipation**) effects and impacts it can offer are potentially beneficial for employee self-esteem and satisfaction. On the other hand, critical approaches identify more subversive, manipulative (see **manipulation**) and detrimental motives and impacts of empowerment initiatives (Sturdy, Grugulis and Willmott, 2001).

Key Words:

Cynicism, Emancipation, Managerialism, Manipulation, Power.

References

Cooke (2004); Hayes and Walsham (2000); Sturdy, Grugulis and Willmott (2001).

Enlightenment

The historical period known as 'The Enlightenment' refers to a period in Western European history during the seventeenth and eighteenth centuries when there was a rapid of expansion of work and ideas in many areas of the arts and sciences. Central to this movement was a focus on reason and the individual as opposed to the more traditional rationales based on aristocratic, societal and religious power bases and identities (see **identity**). The **emergence** of these ideas was not without difficulties and conflict as many of the new ideas presented direct challenges to the central **truths** and beliefs of those traditional bodies. In particular, the domain of *science* matured as a powerful set of disciplines and subdisciplines during this period and this interconnected and catalytically interfaced with the development of the Industrial Revolution in Western Europe.

Equally, the combination of scientific approaches and rationalistic philosophy gave rise to, and underpinned, the subsequent movement termed **Modernism**. The movements and philosophies of Enlightenment and Modernism were to have immense impacts on the evolving and emerging forms of organization in the workplace and society. Linear, positivistic, objectivized, rationalistic (see **linearity**, **positivism**, **objectivity**, **rationalism**) ways of perceiving, understanding and structuring work organization proliferated and dominated factories, offices and workplaces.

It can be argued that, in the contemporary era, with a continuing focus on the metrics of effectiveness and **performativity** across a range of targets, the influence of modernism and rationalism (and the echo of the Enlightenment) is still very apparent. There is, in summary, little doubt that The Enlightenment unleashed extremely powerful forces that still resonate in contemporary workplace (Cummings, 2002; Alvesson and Detz, 2005).

Critical approaches are very mindful of this legacy and many critical texts point up the presence of **modernistic, positivistic, rationalistic** behaviours and structures in organizations while, at the same time, introducing accounts of how people interact with them. In contrast to the **rational** and **objectivized modernistic representations** of organizations, critical approaches and **Critical Management Studies** (CMS) prefer to see how, by way of example, discursive, subjective, emotional and **power** aspects of organizational life have been overlooked (see **discourse**, **subjectivity** and **emotion**).

Key Words:

> The Individual, Linearity, Modernism, Objectivity, Positivism, Rationalism, Religion, Representation, Science.

References

> Alvesson and Deetz (2005); Cummings (2002); Kavanagh (2009); Ten Bos (2005).

Epistemology

'Epistemology' is a term that comes from the Greek word *episteme* which means **knowledge** (i.e. the act of knowing). Epistemology involves understanding of how theories and knowledge are constructed. All research and philosophical comment is based on its chosen or associated epistemological and philosophical stances.

Within **normative** and **mainstream** management and organizational texts, a broadly modernistic (see **modernism**) and positivistic (see **positivism**) position is espoused. **Critical Management Studies** (CMS) has witnessed an extensive expansion in the variety of epistemological positions employed in attempts to develop understanding of organizations including, among many others, **Critical Theory, postmodernism, poststructuralism, social constructionism** and **Critical Realism**. An awareness of epistemology underlines that **knowledge**, and where and how it is constructed, cannot be taken as a neutral given. It is not sufficient to say that knowledge simply *is* or just exists, ready-made and already in place. Knowledge is *made* by people at different times for different purposes and motives. In acknowledging this, it affords opportunities to challenge the assumptions underpinning any knowledge (Maylor and Blackmon, 2005; Bryman and Bell, 2007).

Key Words:

Assumptions, Knowledge, Philosophy.

References

Bryman and Bell (2007); Maylor and Blackmon (2005); Spender and Scherer (2007).

Ethics

Ethics is an aspect of philosophy that is concerned with decisions and choices about what is right and wrong and good and bad. Clearly, what is seen as 'good' for one person may be very 'bad' in the opinion of another person. Ethics is a vast field of study and commentary and it is beyond the scope of a short definition to do full justice to the domain (see for further indicative discussion and illustration Jones, Parker, Ten Bos, 2005).

Organization and management has primarily dedicated its interest to the area of *business ethics*, or, how to conduct business in a consistently ethical manner. Much of the commentary can be deemed as being coached in a **normative** or deterministic (see **determinism**) style of commentary wherein the focus is on identifying sets of rules or guidelines on conduct for managers. Moreover, underlying this is the suspicion by critical approaches (see **Critical Management Studies**) that much of business ethics commentary is disingenuous in that it is interested in doing the 'right' or 'good' thing as long as **performativity** and profits are not endangered.

In relation to ethical issues, critical approaches tend to follow a more *descriptive* rather than *prescriptive* approach. Given the propensity of critical approaches towards, for example, **discourse**, **subjectivity**, **pluralism**, multiple **voices**, **social constructionism**, **postmodernism** and **poststructuralism**, it can be imagined that ideas of **truth**, **reality** good/bad and right/wrong are not so clear-cut. This creates fresh complexities for ethical dilemmas and debates.

Key Words:

Descriptive, Normative, Prescriptive.

References

Jensen, Sandström and Helin (2009); Jones, Parker and Ten Bos (2005); Parker (2003); Ten Bos (2005); Wray-Bliss (2002, 2004).

Ethnography

Ethnography is a research methodology approach that involves the study of groups and communities of people. Ethnography places great importance on studying human interactions in their naturalistic environment (rather than, for example, in a scientific laboratory or artificially created group such as a focus group). Hence, ethnographic types of research frequently employ methods such as **participant observation** and unstructured interviews.

It is quite possible that ethnographic approaches might be located in **mainstream**, **normative**, **managerialist** accounts as much as in critical perspective work. For critical writings, ethnography has an important potential because, as a research methodology, it particularly lends itself to allowing the researcher to observe, for example, **subjective, emotional** (see **subjectivity** and **emotion**) and **lived experience** aspects of the field – aspects which **Critical Management Studies** (CMS) seeks to profile and **privilege** to a greater extent than managerial and **modernistic** accounts. It is worth noting that a worthwhile and valuable conference on ethnographic methodological approaches is run annually at the Management School in Liverpool University in the United Kingdom.

Key Words:

Emotion, Lived Experience, Mainstream, Naturalistic, Normative, Participant Observation, Privilege, Research Methodology, Subjectivity.

References

Alvesson and Deetz (1999); Alvesson and Sköldberg (2009); Bryman and Bell (2007); Humphreys, Brown and Hatch (2003); Kociatkiewicz and Kostera (2010); Van Maanen (1988).

Experience

Experience is central to the human condition and may be described as the events and moments that happen to a person during periods of, or during the course of, his or her life. The human senses, and the ways in which they empirically (see **empiricism**) make experience, intertwined with reflection on those experiences are the central processes of human **sense-making**. People frequently tell **stories** and **narratives** in order to relay experience.

Within organization and management studies the idea of experiential learning has been an enduring concept. Since the mid-1970s and early 1980s this work has been closely associated with the writings of David Kolb (1975, 1983); however, Kolb's work is predominantly couched in a **normative** and **mainstream** frame of reference. **Critical Management Studies** (CMS) has been keen to draw out and discuss what is sometimes termed the **lived experience** aspects of organizational life.

Key Words:

Experiential Learning, Lived Experience, Narrative, Reflection, Sense-making, Stories.

References

Knights and Willmott (1999); Kociatkiewicz and Kostera (2010); Kolb (1983); Kolb and Fry (1975); Sköld (2010).

Ff

Feminism

Feminism encompasses a range of philosophical approaches and a series of social movements and organizations that examine the situation and condition of female gender in society. A central concern of feminism is that women are accorded a lesser position, often cast as the **other**, and oppressed or marginalized by society's **normative power** structures. The extent to which normative structures are male-dominated and controlled is an important feature of these debates. Feminism analyses and comments on these situations and how to redress them by surfacing and acknowledging these issues. It seeks the **emancipation** of women through transformation of the hegemonic discourses, structures and **power** relations that bring them about (see **hegemony**, **discourse** and **structure**).

Writing and commentaries on feminism occupy a vast and complex domain and the surface can only be scratched here; however, significant landmark writings, in addition to many other works, include De Beauvoir's (1949) *Le Deuxième Sexe*, Greer's (1970) *The Female Eunuch* and Wolf's (1990) *The Beauty Myth*. Feminist critiques and approaches have played a significant role in organization and management studies. This work covers a range of issues including the notion and realities of the presence of 'glass ceilings', the use of feminine traits in marketing and organizational **identity**, the career trajectories for women, the implications of feminism for academic discussions such as gender studies and the history and role of the 'mother' figure (Bolton and Boyd 2003; Hopfl 2004).

Key Words:

Emancipation, Freedom, Identity, Marginalized, Normative, Oppressed, Structures.

References

Bolton and Boyd (2003); De Beauvoir's (1949); Gill (2006); Greer (1970); Hopfl (2004); Thomas and Davies (2005).

Flexibility

Flexibility conveys the idea of something being readily or easily changeable. It implies that things can be changed or altered at relatively short notice without too much disruption. Moreover, it suggests that these changes or transitions are manageable by those individuals involved. For companies and managers, flexible working potentially allows them to respond to supply and demand in the marketplace by recruiting labour as and when required on short-term contracts. For employees, flexibility at work is often stated as allowing time to be with family or carry out caring and private responsibilities and activities.

In recent years, the increase in part-time jobs and fixed-term roles is often suggested as offering greater flexibility in the workforce. The **emergence** of more flexible work patterns was largely a consequence and reaction to rigid, heavily unionized work regimes of the post-Second World War era. Thus, flexibility has become a central plank of the modern work environment as the workplace moves from **Fordist** to more **Post-Fordist** forms of working.

However, the downside of flexibility and flexible work patterns is that many of these types of job are located in certain sectors where jobs tend to be low-paid, have long working hours, difficult conditions, poor career prospects and, crucially, insecurity. Examples of such industries typically include leisure, tourism, retail and entertainment. In addition, many of these jobs tend to be held by women, ethnic minorities or people from poor socio-economic circumstances (see **feminism**, **masculinities** and **gender**) (Warhurst, Grugulis and Keep, 2004). Therefore rather than these types of jobs providing freedom to be flexible, they can become poverty traps as people find it difficult to assimilate the means and skills to leave this style of employment for a more permanent, career-focused or developmental role (Thompson and McHugh, 2009).

Key Words:

Career, Changeable, Feminism, Gender, Insecurity, Masculinities, Short Notice.

References

Corona and Godart (2010); Seidl (2007); Thompson and McHugh (2009); Warhurst, Grugulis and Keep (2004); Whittle (2008).

Fordism

The term 'Fordism' describes a method of organizing and managing workplaces. Fordist environments employ highly structured, controlled and systematized environments that are generally geared to mass-production. Within these settings managers are accorded a controlling role and workers are expected to comply with a **unitary** culture and vision that is set by senior managers. Employees are assigned a part of the work in these operations – a specialization of task or labour which is carried out in a repetitive manner. These techniques are aimed at pro-ducing standardized outputs in an effective and efficient manner. The system was made famous by Henry Ford's early car factories which, using Taylorist (see **Taylorism**, **Scientific Management**) principles, developed and honed the concept of Fordism.

Fordist settings are often characterized as **managerialist** and strongly critiqued, by both **Labour Process Theory** and **Critical Management Studies.** It is felt that they are prone to inducing a sense of **alienation** and poor welfare in employees (Carter and Rayner, 1996).

The contemporary business world has needed to respond to con-sumers who increasingly require customized, specialized and flexible responses to their needs and desires (see **flexibility**). Fordism, in its traditional and highly structured mould, is not well disposed to fulfil such a role. This has led the evolution of Fordism towards, for exam-ple, the post-Fordist world of *flexible specialization* (involving small batch production, team cell work groups, lean manufacturing and just-in-time production) (Koch, 2006). Nevertheless, although Fordism may some-times appear to be a work model closely characteristic of the early and mid-twentieth century, this does not mean that its practice and effects are no longer evident. Fordist practices can be witnessed in a range of work environments including, by way of example, call-centres' processes and higher education programming.

Key Words:

Alienation, Critical Management Studies, Labour Process Theory, Managerialism, McDonaldization, Scientific Management, Taylorism.

References

Carter and Rayner (1996); Koch (2006); Peci (2009); Whitley (2003).

Foucauldian

The word 'Foucauldian' derives from the work and the name of the French philosopher Michel Foucault (1926–1984). Although Foucault did not write expressly in relation to the organization and business management fields, his writings broached these spheres and have been adopted by a wide range of scholars. The reference to 'Foucauldian' features, traits or characteristics in a given text frequently alludes to and underscores issues of, among other points, **power**, subjugation, **surveillance**, **identity**, sexuality, **discourse** and **resistance** being in operation.

Key Words:

Discourse, Identity, Power, Resistance, Sexuality, Surveillance.

References

Al-Amoudi (2007); Caldwell (2007); Knights (2004); Rowlinson and Carter (2002); Wray-Bliss (2002).

Also see multiple references to Foucault at the rear of the text.

Functionalism

Functionalism is an approach to constructing and understanding the world in terms of the functions it is intended to, or can, fulfil. Functionalism has a propensity to categorize functions by employing boundaries and delineations (see **boundary** and **linearity**). As such it tends to represent (see **representation**) its subjects in a manner that suggests they are stable and fixed. **Normative** and **mainstream** approach to management and organization are prone to employing and making functionalist frames of reference.

Critical (see **Critical Management Studies** (CMS)) approaches and critiques identify a range of limitations in functionalist views of organization. These centre on issues of the overly **linear**, **reductionist** and contextually over-simplified **representations** they make. Critical approaches tend to draw on alternative philosophical traditions such as **postmodernism** and **poststructuralism.**

Key Words:

Boundaries, Linearity, Reductionist, Representation.

References

Kirkpatrick and Ackroyd (2003); Perrow (2008); Tadajewski (2009a).

Gg

Gaze

The term 'gaze' concerns the act of focusing attention on an object, person(s) or situation and, by doing so, contributing in some way to 'creating' that scene. When a person, or persons, gaze they undertake an act of socially constructing (see **social constructionism**) and **making sense** (see **sense-making**) of what they perceive. In so doing they exercise a moment of **power** as they confer a particular **identity** on the observed site.

Urry (2002), drawing on the case of the business and phenomenon of tourism, has in that particular context identified that having the 'luxury' to gaze in this manner may be an aspirational and identifying modern characteristic of **consumption** and **commodification**. In his analysis he shows how the power to gaze can lift sites and landscapes, for example, 'out of the ordinary'. It is possible to imagine a wide range of workplace contexts in which gazes may construct identity, experience and meaning.

Key Words:

Commodification, Consumption, Identity, Power, Sense-making, Social Constructionism.

References

Roberts (2005); Urry (2002); Woźniak (2010).

Gender

Gender concerns issues surrounding sexual roles, **identity** and **power**. During the course of the twentieth century debates on gender have become increasingly prominent across a range of disciplines and public life. Academic and wider commentary on gender now covers an immense area and a summary is a difficult challenge.

In a historical conventional context it was common to categorize particular professional or domestic roles in relation to masculine or feminine domains. Men were traditionally employed in heavy labouring industries such as steel, ship manufacturing or construction. In this same conventional perspective women carried out office, service (canteen, retail) or domestic roles. Over the last several decades this stereotypical and **boundary**-prone, delineated (see **linearity**) characterization of **gender** roles has changed significantly with individuals with other sexual identities (for example transsexuals and transvestites) undertaking a wide variety of roles across society (see **identity**). This is not at all to say that equal opportunities readily exist for these or other groups. Women are still in a significant proportional minority compared to men in holding posts in senior echelons of business and the professions. There are also frequent reports of certain male groupings, for example young white working-class males and young black males in general, experiencing disadvantages and poor success in employment and education.

Mainstream and **normative** approaches to management have often been charged with presenting an *asexual* (i.e. a world devoid of acknowledging the presence and role of gender) **representation** of the workplace. In contrast to this, **Critical Management Studies** (CMS) approaches have developed a wide range of critiques employing, for example, **postmodernist**, **poststructural**, **deconstructionist** and **Foucauldian** analyses. Such approaches point up the **lived experience** of gender in the workplace addressing issues such as sexual harassment, office romances, sex lives, prejudice, bullying and the way sex and gender may at times be employed (Brewis, 2010). The breadth of work in the area has given rise to the fields of Gender Studies, **Feminism** and **Masculinities** and a range of journals covering the fields (see also: *Gender, Work and Organization* and *Gender in Management: An International Journal*).

Key Words:

Boundary, Disadvantage, Feminism, Gender Roles, Identity, Masculinities, Power, Prejudice, Representation, Stereotyping.

References

Blomberg (2009); Brewis and Linstead (2009); Bowring and Brewis (2009); Murgi and Poggio (2009).

Gestalt

'Gestalt' is the German word for 'form' and the concept of 'wholeness' or 'completeness'. Gestalt originates from the Berlin School of experimental psychology. One of the school students and adherents was Kurt Lewin (1890–1947) who developed a well-known set of models and ideas in relation to change management theory and practice. The term 'Gestalt' is also used to convey the idea of synergy – namely that *the whole is greater than the sum of the parts.*

In critical commentaries, Gestalt is employed periodically in general or generic manner to indicate the rounded, whole, encompassing rich complexity of a situation or issue. The use of the word 'Gestalt' within **Critical Management Studies** (CMS) texts does not necessarily indicate the writer's subscription to the Berlin School's ideological commitments. Rather it is used in a similar manner to other imported foreign **language** terms such as, for example, *zeitgeist* (which alludes to the cultural, political, social, spiritual and ethical spirit of a given time or age) (see **culture**, **politics** and **ethics**).

Key Words:

Synergy, Wholeness.

References

Johnsen and Gudmand-Høyer (2010); Martens (2006).

Hh

Habitus

Habitus can be thought of as the frames of reference or **structures** that shape an individual's mind and thoughts. Each individual will be different with the habitus of his or her mind being structured around varying experiences, memories, tastes, likes, dislikes, feelings, ideas.

Habitus is developed by constant action and reaction to external objective stimuli, artefacts and events (see **objectivity**). Therefore, habitus is subjective in nature but takes on an objectified form produced and reproduced through interaction with particular external environment and influences (see **subjectivity** and **reproduction**). An illustration of this is learning how to be part of a given group or social class. Habitus points at behaviours and ideas which are learned or absorbed from the surrounding context or milieu in which a person predominantly spends time. They are embodied and subsequently re-enacted or reproduced as *learned* behaviours. Although elements of this concept can be traced back through a number of philosophers, it is often the work of French sociologist Pierre Bourdieu (1930–2002) which is commonly cited in critical work (for example, see Mutch, 2003).

Key Words:

Objectivity, Reproduction, Subjectivity.

References

Friedland (2009); Kerr and Robinson (2009); Mutch (2003); Slutskaya and De Cock (2008).

Hegemony (adjective: hegemonic)

Hegemony means when one party or system has dominant control and **power** over another entity or system. It is a term employed in **Critical Management Studies** (CMS) writings to underline relations where, for example, employees or individuals are subjected to an (oppressive) force or power that has influence and control over them. An illustration of such relations is the manager controlling the employee, or, alternatively, a company dominating a particular market or consumer group. Hegemonic **power** relations can lead to bullying and harassment; however, hegemonic effects are not solely physical and psychological and can also be found in a wide range of **discursive** and **symbolic** contexts (see **discourse**).

Hegemony can also exist where a particular philosophical paradigm or perspective dominates. For CMS, **modernistic**, **positivistic**, **mainstream** or **normative** approaches are often seen as the unsatisfactory hegemonic way organizational life is presented (see **modernism** and **positivism**). As an epistemological approach these philosophies are viewed as a hegemonic way of producing **knowledge** (see **epistemology**). However, this is not to exclude or suggest that CMS approaches cannot also exhibit hegemonic effects in certain contexts (see Wray-Bliss, 2004 on this point). For a wide range of CMS critiques, a key purpose is to question, challenge and counter various hegemonic forces and achieve micro-emancipation for the individuals and agents involved (see **emancipation** and **agency**).

Key Words:

Critical Management Studies, Epistemology, Knowledge, Mainstream, Normative, Positivism, Power.

References

Gagliardi (2007); Marens (2010); Wray-Bliss (2004).

Hermeneutics

'Hermeneutics' is a term associated with the study of philosophy. In its broadest, generic sense it concerns the act and art of interpretation of text and the development of an understanding of the processes through which interpretation takes place.

Hermeneutics is a very long-standing area of study and in its original form is closely associated to the study of religious texts and in particular the Old and New Testaments. The development of hermeneutics has taken hermeneutic analysis into wider fields of **discourse, semiotics** (the study of the **meanings** of signs and **symbols**) and **language**.

Hermeneutics does not overtly command a great deal of space within **Critical Management Studies** (CMS) texts. However, the notion of hermeneutics is recognized as an important one that CMS-style commentaries implicitly employ in order to explore subjectivities (see **subjectivity**), **voices** and **boundary delineations** within **postmodern** and **poststructuralist** analyses of work and management contexts (Hatch and Rubin, 2006). Contemporary hermeneutic analyses tend, in general, to accord important weight to context and, in particular, the situation and perspective of the person conducting the analysis or observation (see Vattimo, 1997).

Key Words:

Discourse, Interpretation, Philosophy, Semiotics, Subjectivity, Symbols.

References

Hatch and Rubin (2006); O'Doherty (2008); Robinson and Kerr (2009); Vattimo (1997).

Hierarchy

Hierarchy is a system where different grades, classes or categories (and inherently people or objects within these) are ordered, ranked or positioned in a vertical structure with some groupings being accorded a higher or a lower position and status and authority. The higher the position in the hierarchy, the higher the status and authority.

Max Weber's (1864–1920) famous study analysed the role of **authority** and **bureaucracy** in relation to hierarchy.

There is a substantial body of commentary on hierarchy and hierarchical forms and issues in organization and management. The **normative** view of hierarchy is that top and upper levels have the responsibility and the **power** to set the strategic vision and work out the related strategy that the organization will follow. The middle tiers of the hierarchy are responsible for conveying and implementing this vision in the lower or operational employee areas. A typical metaphor for this is the upper level 'head and brain' sections guiding the body and limbs that are the 'doing' or manual sections of the firm.

Hierarchy is still a commonplace structure in contemporary organizations and has developed in many ways since the early bureaucratic (see **bureaucracy**) forms discussed by Weber to embrace various forms of departmentalization, divisionalization and various degrees of centralization and decentralization. Within all of these forms, notions of the role and potential for **empowerment**, **resistance** and flows of **power** other than those from the top of the hierarchy downwards have been pointed up in number of critical critiques.

Key Words:

Authority, Bureaucracy, Empowerment, Power, Resistance.

References

Blomberg (2009); Mutch (2005).

Human Relations

The term 'Human Relations' derives from the Human Relations School based at Harvard University and was developed by the leading scholar Elton Mayo (1880–1949) during the inter-war and post-Second World War periods. In particular, it was the Hawthorne Studies carried out at the Hawthorne works of the Western Electric Company in Chicago which provided great impetus and wider awareness of the School's work.

Human Relations is particularly interested in developing organizations by studying and bringing about changes in employee behaviour at work. Mayo's work showed that social dimensions and interaction at work are important and should not be overlooked. Equally, he felt that it was vital that managers recognize this and work in **non-mechanistic** manners to improve work atmospheres and thereby productivity.

While Human Relations has not been a **hegemonic** or powerful influence on CMS approaches, its attempts to better understand the human condition and the role of social interaction in workplaces have nevertheless made it an occasional valuable point of reference and part of a wider historical background context (Linstead, Fulop and Lilley, 2009).

Key Words:

Hawthorne, Mayo, Non-mechanistic.

References

Higgins and Tamm-Hallström (2007); Linstead, Fulop and Lilley (2009); O'Connor (1999).

Humanist (approaches)

This approach is concerned with the notion of human **identity** and 'self' being placed at the centre of the human condition with the purpose of focusing on developing human growth and potential. Therefore, central to the humanist approach is the notion of the (actual) self and the idealized self and the journey to reconcile these two positions. Humanism is not necessarily a dominant influence on **Critical Management Studies** (CMS) approaches; however, CMS does engage in related commitments towards attempts at **emancipation** in the workplace and life in general.

Key Words:

Emancipation, Human Potential.

References

Caldwell (2007); Clegg, Kornberger and Pitsis (2008); Johnsen and Gudmand-Høyer (2010).

Humour

Humour refers to a person's general mood disposition and condition or alternatively a spat of joking that causes people to laugh or be amused and which happens spontaneously and without particular planning. Humour forms a social glue that brings people together. In its latter sense, humour can offer a form of **resistance** against **authority** or **managerialism**. Furthermore, it might aim to relieve boredom and create interest in the work environment. Humour is frequently rendered in accounts of organizations and management through **stories** and **narratives**.

Key Words:

Narratives, Resistance, Stories.

References

Gabriel (2000); Rhodes and Westwood (2008); Watson (2006).

Hypermodernity

The term 'hypermodernity' is a composite of hyper and modernity. Hyper generally means excessive, or over and beyond. Modernity (see **modernism**) is a perspective bound up with a mechanistic, progress-orientated, science and technology underpinned view of the world. To label a period or an event hypermodernity points at an intensification, deepening and speeding up of modernistic characteristics, within the new challenges of the late twentieth and twenty-first centuries. In particular, hypermodernity is connected to the idea of ever-expanding human understanding and control and envisages the positive and progressive effects of the merger of different forms of technical and medical/scientific knowledge. Clearly, states of hypermodernity also have downsides and problems.

Key Words:

Intensification, Modernism, Science, Technology.

References

Armitage (2002); Armitage and Roberts (2002); Lipovetsky and Charles (2005).

Hyper-reality

'Hyper-reality' literally means 'greater or more real than reality' – an intense and heightened state of **reality**. There arrives a point where this hyper-reality becomes so 'real' as to replace notional everyday perceptions of reality and thereby create *simulacra* – simulations that are effectively more real than reality. The French philosopher Jean Baudrillard (1929–2007) was a central exponent of this thinking. The **normative** and positivistic (see **positivism**) idea of an objective (see **objectivity**) and solid unchangeable object about which information and **language** are employed is replaced and displaced by signs and **symbols** to create a new reality – a hyper-reality. In such a state or world, the signs do not refer back to some original object but go on to refer to other and further signs. Baudrillard underlined the role of the press, mass media and communications in assisting this state of affairs.

Key Words:

Baudrillard, Reality, Simulacra, Symbols.

References

Baudrillard (1975, 1983); Hjorth and Pelzer (2007); Terashima and Tiffin (2001).

Hypothesis (plural: hypotheses)

A hypothesis is a proposal regarding what may constitute a '**truth**' or 'fact'. More popularly expressed, it is a 'hunch' about what might be the case or the truth.

IIypotheses are used as part of the positivistic (see **positivism**), scientific, experimentalist approach to developing **knowledge** (see **epistemology**). As part of that process a given hypothesis might be proved correct or incorrect. It does not matter that it is proven incorrect since, in itself, this too offers knowledge just as important regarding what 'is not' as well as 'what is'. Within the experimentationalist, (i.e. science-based) epistemological (see **epistemology**) approach, repeatedly proven and interrelated hypothesis are used to begin to build **theory**.

Normative, managerialist (see **managerialism**) approaches are commonly built on **positivistic** and hypothesis building stances whereas **Critical Management Studies** (CMS) approaches tend to be cautious and more ambivalent regarding claims about the solidity or concrete nature of 'truths' or 'facts'. In CMS, the researcher, however inadvertently or deliberately, reflexively (see **reflexivity**) and subjectively (see **subjectivity**) is seen as playing a role in creating those 'truths' and 'facts' and therefore is less prone to use the **language** and techniques of hypotheses.

Key Words:

Epistemology, Objectivity, Positivism, Subjectivity, Theory, Truth.

References

Bryman and Bell (2007); Miettinen and Virkkunen (2005).

Identity

Attempts at understanding identity have been extensive in the history of philosophy involving work by, for example, Plato (428–427 BC), Liebnitz (1646–1716) Hume (1711–1776), Locke (1632–1704) and Wittgenstein (1889–1951). Identity is a central concept not only in **Critical Management Studies** (CMS) but also in wider social, political and psychological spheres (see **politics**). Identity concerns association of a person or entity with particular or distinctive characteristics, values and beliefs.

In **spatial** terms, identity can be seen as a physical attribute or feature relating to an individual or some form of collective of individuals. Equally, it could refer to an entity such as an organization. In **temporal** terms, identity involves, for example, beliefs, attitudes, **ethics**, **politics** that can transform over time as new meanings are negotiated by, or for, the person or entity. **Narrative** plays a central role in the negotiation of identity in terms of how people, groups and even entities such as organizations tell **stories**, **socially construct** and **represent** themselves and **others**. Studies pointing at these processes have been a long-standing focus in organization and management contexts (by way of illustration, see Goffman, 1959; Sims, Pullen and Beech, 2007; Du Gay and Elliott, 2008). This engagement has led to the expression 'identity work' which underlines the active complex and ongoing labour that many people pursue in cultivating and developing their own and others' identities. Identity affords the opportunity to distinguish what is similar and what is different. Equally, identity can be something that is used to align and relate to, for example, similar people in a group, or shared experiences, and activities (members of a club).

In CMS-influenced discussions, identities are, in **ontological** terms, likely to be viewed as being in transition or in transformation rather than being fixed or unchanging (see **ontology**). This may seem a reasonable assumption given **empirical** evidence (see **empiricism**) on how human beings **experience** or engineer changes in their work role or personality during the course of their life or, alternatively, in the way a company undergoes branding and image changes during its history. Even though this perpetually shifting state may characterize discussions on identity within much CMS **discourse**, the ability to debate identity nevertheless requires **representation** even if it is a question of describing transforming patterns. This often contrasts with **normative** or **managerialist** accounts of identity which generally do not problematize notions of identity. Rather, managerialist accounts tend to take identity as something constituted of a less problematic and more fixed and given nature. In the case of organizations, identity is built up and maintained and often attempted to be passed on to employees in the form of **corporate culture**, vision or values. Issues of organizational identity now stretch far beyond the surface notion of communicating or promoting image. It is an organization-wide organic project of formal and informal identity negotiation and presentation.

The negotiation and development of identity can be viewed as a political act, involving difficult choices and alignments (see **politics**). These processes may involve people or groups of people feeling coerced or cajoled into assuming particular behaviours or adopting certain language. This apparent **McDonaldization** of identity has emerged as a serious concern in a range of corporate settings. Organizations often show a great propensity to develop and maintain identities. Logos, tradenames, trademarks, symbols, images on buildings, uniforms in corporate literature are physical items that go to produce, sustain and reinforce this identity. Indeed, organizational identity is embraced in a legal framework. Organizations have boundaries circumscribed around them and their activities by law which determines what the organization is allowed to do and what it is not (see **boundary**). Aspects of the presentation and **representation** of identity will be in documents such as the Memorandum of Association.

In conclusion, it is important to reiterate that for critical perspectives, identity is seen as operating more or less in an ongoing state of forming and reforming – even if in the interludes between these phases the impression is received that identity is fixed. Parts of identity are being left behind while others are being assumed and constructed. This means that while certain aspects of identity, whether for a person or an organization, may be temporally enduring, they are also potently related to and informed by the given context(s) in which they are situated.

Key Words:

Boundary, Discourse, McDonaldization, Other, Representation, Spatial, Stories, Temporal.

References

Du Gay and Elliott (2008); Du Gay, Evans and Redman (2000); Fineman, Gabriel and Sims (2010); Goffman (1959); Mills, Helms Mills and Thomas (2004); Sims, Pullen and Beech (2007).

Ideology

The grouping or system of ideas that underpins and drives a particular political or economic viewpoint is termed an *ideology* (see **politics**). An ideology embraces an internally coherent set of ideas, theories (see **theory**) and assumptions. In this regard, it is possible, for example, to see **modernism**, **positivism** and **managerialism** as possessing particular ideological characteristics. Adherence to, and belief in, a particular ideology is likely to lead to, or purportedly justify, particular choices and actions. For example, adherents to a **managerialist** ideology may see optimum **performativity** as of paramount importance to their ideological integrity. In turn, this may be felt to justify severe measures such as reshaping and restructuring the organization through forced redundancies and job role reallocation even this may mean hardship for many people.

On a broader historical canvas it should be noted that ideological differences can lead to major conflicts. This is exemplified by the battles waged in the Second World War by liberal democracies (the USA, Britain and their allies) against fascist, militaristic axis regimes (Germany, Italy and Japan). In particular within this conflict, the battle between allied Communist Soviet Russia and German fascist National Socialism (Nazism) was a particularly vicious politically ideologically rooted aspect of the confrontation. The Second World War led onto the subsequent **Cold War** between the West and the USSR which perpetuated ideological oppositions on the world stage.

In the ongoing contemporary era, the term 'ideology' has, in popular terms, been increasingly cast in a negative light, or as a pejorative term, indicating dogma and die-hard adherence to old, faded or mis-guided ideas and ideals. To a large extent, in the Western World, Marxism can be said to have has experienced this effect in recent decades.

Ideologies, such as **managerialism**, have marked differences to, and are frequently challenged by, alternative approaches such as **Critical Management Studies** (CMS). However, it is difficult, if not impossible, to portray CMS as an entirely coherent and **unitary** ideology. CMS is the result of the coming together and sourcing of ideas and materials from a vast range of sources. Consequently, it is sometimes difficult to reconcile the ideological commitments and characteristics of these various contributions (see Adler, Forbes and Willmott, 2007; Clegg, Kornberger, Carter and Rhodes, 2006; Fournier and Grey, 2000).

Key Words:

Critical Management Studies, Managerialism, Theory.

References

Adler, Forbes and Willmott (2007); Clegg, Kornberger, Carter and Rhodes (2006); Fournier and Grey (2000); Rehn (2008).

Impression management

As individuals we are constantly aware of the opinions people may be forming about us during the course of our interactions with them. We do not necessarily allow these impressions to form independently but, often, we will say things or take action to try to ensure a particular view of us is more likely to be formed than another. This is termed 'impression management' (Goffman, 1959; Rosenfeld, Giacalone and Riordan, 2002).

It is possible to see how issues of **power, language, discourse, identity** may all play a role in the processing of impression management. Some individuals may well be more proficient than others at using the clues and cues of creating a 'good' or required impression.

Key Words:

Discourse, Identity, Language, Power.

References

Rosenfeld, Giacalone and Riordan (2002); Goffman (1959); Whittle (2008).

Inductivism

Inductivism is a methodological stance and approach in which the researcher gathers data on a research topic or area and then, through various iterative analytical processes and techniques, identifies salient characteristics and traits from the data. Inductivism embodies the idea that subjective processes (see **subjectivity**) play a significant role in the creation of 'facts' and information.

Inductivism contrasts with **deductivism**. In the latter, a **hypothesis**, or in other words a possible belief about a **truth**, regarding an **objectively** framed fact that already 'exists out there' is attempted to be proved or disproved thereby weakening or strengthening the **hypothesis**. However, with inductivism, the hypothesis or theory is slowly built up and constructed around the profile or **story** that the data and reports from the research respondents (i.e. the people or situation being researched) are gradually portraying to the researcher(s).

In the main, critical approaches employ inductivist-style methodological viewpoints rather than **objectivity**-valuing **deductivist** perspectives. Inductivist-style approaches are suspicious of the possibility of attaining purely objective judgements in making sense of research settings as individual human interpretation and **social construction** are potentially always in play (see **sense-making**). They tend to adopt an approach that values subjective complexities of human interaction and **sense-making** thereof (see **subjectivity**). Deductive, **positivist** approaches are conventionally more commonly employed in **mainstream** and **normative** approaches to management and organization.

Key Words:

Deductivism, Hypothesis, Objectivity, Subjectivity.

References

Bryman and Bell (2007); Jankowicz (2005); Kuhn (2009); Silverman (2010); Whittle (2008).

Institution (adjective: institutional)

An institution is an organization set up for a particular purpose based on, for example, an educational, economic, religious, research or social objective. A substantial body of knowledge has developed in relation to *institutional theory* which argues that organizations develop the shapes they evolve into primarily due to cultural reasons (see **culture**). This occurs through *institutional* **isomorphism** (i.e. wherein organizations develop similar structures but for different origins and reasons). In other words, institutions and organizations are not instigated 'ready-made' – rather they emerge (see **emergence**), evolve and *become* the institutions they are.

Institutions, and the form they take, have a major influence on the people who work in, and in connection with, them. Equally, and reciprocally, through processes of, for example, **social constructionism** within communities of employees and managers, patterns and cultures of given institutions will be produced and reproduced (see **reproduction**). Similarly, this effect will also be produced by individuals from institutions in given business sectors meeting at conferences and seminars and sharing ideas and impressions. The way in which **knowledge** develops in, and between, institutions constitutes a substantial part of the field in terms of both *knowledge management*, sharing strategies and *fashions, fads and trends* in organization and management. *Neo-institutionalism* (or new institutionalism) tends to dedicate more emphasis on issues of **power** in relation to building **trust** within institutions and organizations and is particularly interested in highlighting the ephemeral nature of trust borne out of conflict or **power**.

Key Words:

Power, Social Constructionism, Trust.

References

Di Maggio and Powell (2002); Greenwood, Olivier, Suddaby and Sahlin-Andersson (2008); Hanlon (2004).

Interpretivism

Interpretivism is a methodological approach which seeks to understand the subjective **meanings** and **sense-making** that are emerging from a given field under research. Interpretivism and variations of this approach are widely used in critical work (see **Critical Management Studies (CMS)**). It is a broad term that encompasses a wide range of approaches that **privilege subjectivity** rather than objectivity. Interpretivism is often **ontologically** and **epistemologically** contrasted with approaches such as **deductivism** and **positivism** which prize **objectivity**.

Key Words:

Epistemology, Meaning, Ontology, Positivism, Privilege, Subjectivity.

References

Allard-Poesi (2005); Bryman and Bell (2007); Jankowicz (2005).

Isomorphism

'Isomorphism' is a term originally derived from the natural sciences. In biological terms it indicates an organism that has a similar appearance to other organisms even though their make-up or composition is actually different.

This concept has been applied to organization theory to point at how organizations evolve to look similar to one another yet their origins and journeys are, in fact, quite distinct (Di Maggio and Powell, 2002). This idea is a central idea of what is termed *Institutional Theory* (see **institution** and **theory**).

In organizations, isomorphism is often talked about in three ways: **normative**, coercive and **mimetic**. **Normative** isomorphism incorporates those practices that become commonplace in organizations because, for various reasons, they are seen as a good thing to do. Illustrations of this might be use of hot-desking, just-in-time, best-practice, dress-down Fridays and so on. Coercive isomorphism is when all organizations are obligated to do something, such as following the law relating to their area of operation. **Mimetic** isomorphism occurs when people in an organization choose to copy the practice of another organization. This form of competitive behaviour is likely to be influenced by, among other things, management and organizational fads and fashions (see **impression management**).

Key Words:

Coercive, Institutional Theory, Mimetic, Normative.

References

Alvarez, Mazza and Pedersen (2005); Di Maggio and Powell (2002); Lawrence and Phillips (2004).

Jj Kk Ll

Knowledge

A considerable amount of attention has been paid in various literatures, historically and contemporaneously, as to what constitutes knowledge and how it is formed. Knowledge is, in part, about the awareness and familiarity individuals have with a given subject or sphere. It can also be connected with the idea of knowledge giving rise to information (i.e. creating more knowledge) and also the idea of being able to think of our total, or sum, knowledge – what one, or a group, is aware of regarding a topic or issue.

The process through which knowledge is made is an epistemological issue (see **epistemology**). In general, the interpretivistic, inductive (see **interpretivism, inductivism**) **subjectivity**-orientated approach of critical perspectives means that it is very engaged with analysing the ways in which issues around knowledge are constructed and sense is created for individuals and groups (see **social constructionism** and **sense-making**).

In more **normative** or **mainstream** presentations it is more common to develop binary or **dualistic** views of knowledge such as, for example, *tacit* (unwritten, based on custom and practice) or *explicit* **knowledge** (written plans, diagrams, policies etc.) (Nonaka and Takeuchi, 1995). Alternatively, as a further illustration, it is common to talk of *experiential* **knowledge** (knowledge derived from doing things, taking actions) (Kolb, 1984) as opposed to knowledge gleaned through instruction.

The term 'knowledge' has given rise to further terms such as the *knowledge economy* and *knowledge management*. The knowledge economy is a post-industrial form of economic landscape and activity. This is based on tertiary sector services (including tourism, financial, education and insurance) rather than primary industries such as coalmining or secondary industries like heavy industry and manufacturing (see **Modernism**, **Fordism**, **Postmodernism**). Knowledge, and the management of that knowledge (using, for example, expert systems, expert knowledge workers), is central to the knowledge economy. This is a world in transition and **Critical Management Studies** (CMS) has taken great interest in how issues of, for example, **identity** and **power** play out in relation to it (Alvesson and Robertson, 2006; Scarbrough et al., 2007a, 2007b).

Key Words:

Epistemology, Experiential Knowledge, Explicit Knowledge, Knowledge Economy, Knowledge Management, Post-Industrial, Tacit Knowledge.

References

Alvesson and Robertson (2006); Kolb (1983); Nonaka and Takeuchi (1995); Scarbrough et al (2007a, 2007b).

Labour Process Theory (LPT)

Labour Process theory (LPT) is a movement and a body of thought that focuses on industrial relations, industrial sociology and work psychology. Its origins draw extensively on Marxist, socialist and left-wing **ideology** and writings. The early formation of LPT was strongly influenced by Braverman's (1974) work which pointed up how deskilling, loss of **identity** and **alienation** were emerging as serious issues in the modern workplace (see **emergence** and **modernism**). As a development to Braverman's work, later accounts from within LPT have pointed up the multifarious manners in which employees undertake forms of **resistance** in the workplace in response to **managerialism**.

LPT was one of the strands of work from which **Critical Management Studies** (CMS) emerged. CMS has since evolved in myriad manners and it is no longer closely kindred with LPT. Some LPT adherents take serious issue with the postmodern and poststructuralist (see **postmodernism** and **poststructuralism**) allegiances and connections evident from certain quarters of CMS signalling such studies as an irrelevant deviation and indulgence rather than a serious attempt to understand and emancipate workers (see **emancipation**) (Thompson,

1993). Equally, some CMS commentators find the underlying Marxist **dualism** in LPT to exhibit **reductionist**, oversimplified and archaic traits in the face of what CMS commentators may see as a radically transformed and ever-changing world. LPT has a long-running and regular United Kingdom-based academic conference.

Key Words:

Alienation, Critical Management Studies, Ideology, Managerialism, Resistance.

References

Braverman (1974); Carey (2009); Sewell (2005); Thompson (1993); Wray-Bliss (2002).

Language

Language is commonly thought of as the means through which animals and human beings communicate. The topic of language is one that is vast and is addressed through a wide range of disciplines, not least of all, philosophy, linguistics and sociology.

Language has emerged as a centrally important aspect of many critiques and commentaries in **Critical Management Studies** (CMS) particularly in relation to **discourse**. Key philosophical sources include, among others, Michel Foucault, Jacques Derrida and Francois Lyotard. Through postmodern and poststructuralist (see **postmodernism** and **poststructuralism**) approaches, by way of illustration, Foucault investigated how language operates in relation to **knowledge** and **power**; Derrida analysed how language can be deconstructed (see **deconstructionism**) so that implicit meaning cannot be assigned to or determined from a text; Lyotard discussed the role of *grand narratives* or **meta-narratives** in **sense-making** in the contemporary and modernistic era (see **modernism** and **narrative**).

The use of **narratives** and **stories** across the span of **mainstream**, **normative** and **CMS** has challenged the concept of language as being neutral. It should be noted however that **mainstream** and **normative** approaches to organization and business management are unlikely to subject language and discourse to the same intensive scrutiny and interpretation as a **CMS** perspective-driven approach.

Key Words:

Discourse, Knowledge, Mainstream, Narratives, Normative, Power, Stories.

References

Fay (2008); Taylor and Robichaud (2004); Tietze, Cohen and Musson (2003).

Legitimation

Legitimation and legitimacy, in the broadest sense, concern when something is seen as lawful, proper, regular and probably affirmed by some protocol, procedure or approval. The distinction of coercion or coerced **power**, as contrasted with legitimate power, is frequently made.

With regard to organizations and managing, legitimacy might, for instance, be viewed as the right to manage and be respected as a manager – clearly a critical and important issue for an organization to be able to function in a reasonable manner. From a **normative** or **mainstream** management perspective, managers, as a consequence of the position they hold in the **hierarchy** or **structure**, are seen as legitimate to manage or lead. Even within a mainstream **representation** of the legitmation of relations in the firm, this is a view that might be challenged by employees from time to time or, for example, representatives of employees such as trades unions.

Legitimation is inextricably linked with issues of **authority** and **power**. Critical approaches are particularly interested in critiquing (**normative**) portrayals, and analysing the nature of legitimacy and the political, cultural and symbolic ways in which it is produced and reproduced in a range of contexts (see **politics**, **culture**, **symbolism** and **reproduction**).

Key Words:

Hierarchy, Mainstream, Normative, Representation, Structure.

References

De Clerq and Voronov (2009); Sturdy, Clark, Fincham and Handley (2009).

Linearity (adjective: linear)

The term *linear* pertains to lines and the characteristics of lines. Lines are frequently declared in a given domain or topic in order to dissect or categorize an area and thereby facilitate analysis and understanding. In this manner, the lines delineate one area from another thereby inviting analyses of comparison and contrast.

Accounts of management and organization that might be termed, from the point of view of critical commentators, **normative**, **positivistic**,

managerialist or **mainstream**, are often purported to display a number of characteristics in the manner in which they discuss and address issues. Typically, these charges tend to centre on concerns about the **objective**, **rationalistic** and sanitized manner in which these accounts are elaborated. In tandem, there tends to be a cause-and-effect, **deterministic**, assumption underlying many mainstream accounts that one event, stage or process leads to another in a straightforward and unproblematic manner. An illustration of this might be line diagrams, charts and two-by-two box grid diagrams in the subject areas of marketing or strategic planning. These seem to imply a world that is (artificially) divided into neat boxes, categories and areas. In this way, **normative** and **mainstream** accounts are often described as *linear* in nature.

Critical approaches often find linear **representations** of managerial and organizational life problematic and poor in contextual richness they offer. The delineation of the frequent messiness of human contact is felt to require an appreciation of more subjective approaches that draw out and recognize blurring of alleged boundaries and categories (see **boundary** and **subjectivity**). 'Linear', 'linearity' or 'delineation' are not terms or areas of study in themselves as such, but they do constitute three related terms that are occasionally employed in a generic manner in critical texts.

Key Words:

Boundaries, Mainstream, Normative, Objectivity, Rationality, Subjectivity.

References

Peci (2009); Slack and Hinings (2004).

Lived experience

The concept of lived experience revolves around attempts to develop a deeper and richer understanding of how an individual or group make sense of life and the events, structures and relationships that constitute their experiences (see **experience** and **sense-making** (Weick, 1995)). Lived experience is interested in attaining a portrayal of organizational life and this is seen as being in stark contrast to many of the often dry, sterile and anodyne **representations** offered in **normative** and **mainstream** textbooks.

Within **Critical Management Studies** (CMS), the idea was given particular prominence in Knights and Willmott's (1999) work *Management Lives: Power and Identity in Work Organizations*. In order to identify a resource that could offer a more lively **representation** of organizational life, Knights and Willmott accessed novels in which the plots were set extensively in organizational and managerial contexts. These included David Lodge's *Nice Work* (1988), Tom Wolfe's *The Bonfire of the Vanities* (1987) and Milan Kundera's *The Unbearable Lightness of Being* (1984). Knights and Willmott demonstrate how, through the novel's characters, plots, **stories** and **narratives** we can witness and identify the panoply of human fallibilities and triumphs.

Although use of the term is occasionally witnessed in academic papers (and not only in CMS-oriented works), commentary invoking 'lived experience' is not overly extensive. It has rather become a touchstone term that is used to appeal for, or point to, a more dynamic way of talking about human experience that supposedly contrasts with (non-CMS style) normative, **reductionist**, **positivistic** and **managerialist** representations.

In CMS contexts, challenges could be raised against the validity of the concept of lived experience suggesting that it is, in fact, in its own way **representationalist**. Such a view would claim that lived experience is *essentialist* in that it aims to 'capture' and 'contain' experiences through its descriptions. Ironically, in so doing it potentially impedes achievement of the precise thing it is seeking to achieve – namely provide a living, dynamic, organic and vibrant portrayal of a setting or series of events. The core of such critiques of lived experience is that from the moment the vast richness and complexity of human experiences is labelled and boxed off (i.e. **represented**) in lived experience portrayals they may become frozen and calcified acting like fixed case studies and hence losing their capacity and potential for endless interpretation. Nevertheless, such criticisms perhaps overlook the necessity to have some rich and insightful means, or vehicle, of discussing human experience. The very fact that we attempt to represent experience through **language** is an unavoidable act and novels, **narrative** and **stories** provide multi-dimensional and evocative ways of moving towards this (Eastmond, 2007).

Key Words:

Narrative, Novels, Reductionism, Representation, Sense-making, Stories.

References

Eastmond (2007); Knights and Willmott (1999); McCabe (2007); O'Doherty (2008); Weick (1995); Zhang, Spicer and Hancock (2008).

Mm

Mainstream

'Mainstream' means the prevailing view or opinion. It might also designate the dominant or hegemonic state of affairs (see **hegemony**) with regards to a particular sphere or area.

The term 'mainstream' is commonly employed in **Critical Management Studies** (CMS) writings. It is intended to convey writings that adopt a modernistic, rationalistic, linear and positivistic stance in the way they portray and discuss organization and management (see **modernism**, **rationality**, **linearity** and **positivism**). Critical perspective writings often take issue with mainstream accounts of managerial and organizational life. CMS, by employing a range of philosophical sources, influences and analytical frames of reference, frequently points up the **reductionist** and emotionally devoid nature of these **normative** portrayals of organizational life. In contrast, CMS tends to sponsor a more, for example, discursive, emergent, non-representationlist or '**lived experience**' approach (see Knights and Willmott, 2007: 40) (see **discourse**, **emergence** and **representation**).

'Mainstream' is not a technical term in CMS, rather it is a generic (almost, on occasion, stereotypical) label used broadly to allude to non-CMS approaches. Often, it is not explicitly examined but taken for granted as a given against which CMS approaches can be compared and contrasted. This, perhaps on occasion, casual treatment of mainstream approaches by CMS is in itself a point worthy of further examination by critical perspective writings.

Key Words:

Linearity, Modernism, Positivism, Rationalism.

References

Corbett (1995); Hotho and Pollard (2007); Knights and Willmott (2007).

Manager

Traditionally, a manager is viewed as a person who is charged with, and responsible for, controlling and directing actions and activities within, or in relation to, an organization, process or project. It is a truism, but nevertheless important here to state, that the literature and materials on managers and management is vast, constantly expanding and therefore almost immeasurable and certainly very difficult to summarize in brief terms (Drucker, 1954; Watson, 2006; Linstead, Fulop and Lilley, 2009).

The purpose here, therefore, is to provide an immediate overview of a number of pertinent issues from which future exploration can be undertaken.

Managers are at the heart, indeed often the central character, of much business and organization commentary. This covers topics, by way of the most superficial rendering, such as: types of managers (i.e. middle, top, senior managers etc.), managerial work patterns, manager **identity**, managers and **power**, manager roles in relation to **structure**, ethical challenges for managers and so on and so forth (see **ethics**). In other ways, managers might be seen as a cultural or social grouping or even elite (see **culture**).

Critical perspective analyses and commentaries, perhaps in part because of their liberal/left-wing socialist and Marxist influences (also see **Labour Process Theory**, **Marxism** and **Capitalism**), have, particularly in early studies, cast managers and managerial regimes as a **power** figure in relation to which **resistance** may occur. However, in contrast, stemming from a range of studies in and around the early 1990s (see for example, Watson's 1994 *In Search of Management*) critically influenced accounts increasingly tended towards researching and portraying the replete human dimensions and **experiences** of being a manager rather than simplistically casting the manager as the **other**.

Key Words:

Identity, Labour Process Theory, Marxism, Other, Power, Resistance, Structure.

References

Drucker (1954); Linstead, Fulop and Lilley (2009); Thomas and Linstead (2002); Watson (1994, 2006).

Managerialism

For critical commentators 'managerialism' is employed as a broad term intended to represent dissatisfaction with particular managerial behaviour and practices. In this way, managerialism is cast as a negative phenomenon and is discussed in questioning and even pejorative terms. Such critiques point up managerialism as behaviour and environments which condone and sponsor robotic and automaton-like behaviour by managers prone to being overly focused on outputs and performance issues with little regard or sensitivity for employees' and individuals' social and human dimensions. In those instances where human aspects are addressed, they are likely to be treated with formulaic 'soft-skills' solutions which tend to produce a collateral series of negative effects and impacts. This can give rise to management actions seeming patronizing, dismissive and disingenuous as well as damaging. Equity or social justice tends not to be a primary concern of managerialistic behaviour. In this light, it might be argued as a philosophy whose slogan is 'the ends justify the means'. Here, the 'ends' are efficiency and effectiveness in the achievement of conventional capitalistic (see **capitalism** and **Marxism**) targets and metrics centred on maximization of, for example, profit, cost-savings and market share. The 'means' are an altogether different matter and managerialist settings are often charged with spin, duplicity and self-serving expediency.

Managerialism is therefore a way of 'being' for many of the individuals bound up in such 'worlds'. It verges on the point of being an **ideology** in that it offers a series of ideas of how to be and how to behave. Critics of managerialism may find this a thin philosophy to guide a person's life and it is therefore not surprising that comedy and satire have been levelled at managerialist behaviour. In particular, we might think of the characters of Gordon Brittas in the *Brittas Empire* (BBC1 1991–1997) or David Brent in the British television comic drama *The Office* (BBC2 2001–2003) as incisive parodies of managerialist **language** and behaviour. Exponents of managerialist approaches are likely to employ 'management speak' – a managerialistic discursive (see **discourse**) repertoire of which well-rehearsed and illustrative examples include, 'let's look at these issues going forward', ' ... we need to think outside the box ... ', 'we need to get our ducks in a row ... ', 'we need to empower our staff ... ' and so on and so forth – the phraseology is extensive and invasive.

Indeed, so pervasive is this phenomenon that it has become 'noticed' by a wider public and has given rise to a considerable degree of wariness and **resistance** against this way of talking. Some commentators have even discussed the idea of covertly playing a 'buzzword' or 'bullshit bingo' game in work meetings. Here, prior to the meeting, employees secretly draw up bingo cards of 'management speak' and try to be the first person to spot managerialist terms used so they can be crossed off and the 'bingo' game won!

Like much of the way of seeing the world to which managerialism belongs there is little or no reflexive or self-aware dimension to its practice or its use of **language**. Simply stated, managerialism does not realize it is managerialist. While critical perspectives view managerialism as an attempt to create and sustain oppressive, undesirable and unuseful ways of being, managerialism and its exponents would be unlikely to question it. It is simply propagated and propagandized as *the* way rather than *a* way to work with and in organizations. It is resiliently unquestioning of the body of **normative** managerialist **knowledge** from which it draws its guidance. It can thus be seen that managerialistic behaviour frequently comes with a high degree of arrogance and superiority regarding its own merits. And, it can be surmised that many managerialistic **managers** would almost never engage the term 'managerialist' as a descriptive term – it is invisible to them. As noted at the outset, this is a label employed almost uniquely in the critical realm. The use of 'managerialism' labels as problematic processes of **reification** of **managers** and the role of **managers** in organizations and indeed wider society and the attempt to assert managers and manager **identity** as an elite. An extension of this trend is that certain managers or business figures may even be projected as role models for non-business type environments that is 'celebrity' or guru managers or business people.

The values and ideas of (**normative**) 'management' provide managers with the apparent prerogative to control activities within organizations. It is therefore inevitably bound up with issues of **power**, who controls it and associated organizational **politics**. Let us be clear, for managerialistically minded people, **power** and the exercise of **power** *are* central objectives. Through the use of managerial power, in order to establish resource planning, allocation and monitoring, managerialism is unquestioningly convinced that the most efficient, effective and modern practices, leading to optimal outputs and outcomes, can and *will* be achieved. The use of the term 'modern' here has a number of inflections. Many managers would be flattered and indeed are likely to proclaim explicitly the ambition to see themselves as 'modernizing' and progressive. However, for critical perspectives, this gives rise to an ironic linguistic twist wherein 'modern' is associated with **modernism** and **modernity.** These are seen as environments dominated by an ethos which is often associated with scientific, objectified, linear ways of seeing and representing the world (see **objectivity, linearity** and **representation**).

Managerialistic behaviour is focused on action. It views itself as dynamic in relation, and in contrast, to the alleged inert and underperforming environments in which it operates. In the contemporary era, managerialism has frequently been proffered as a solution to restructuring and improving organizations seen as bureaucratic and slow to react. Stereotypically these traits have been associated with public sector bodies (especially the Health Service, the Civil Service, police forces and emergency services) and so it is no surprise to find extensive writings and cases variously promoting and challenging the application of managerialist techniques to these areas and the emergence of what is termed 'New Public Sector Management' (Clarke, Gerwitz and McLaughlin, 2000).

For critical perspectives, there may well be a degree of danger in developing and constructing **meanings** and critiques around all-encompassing terms such as 'managerialism'. By the repeated use of 'managerialism' as a generic condemnatory label, critical debate risks losing its potency of critique and slipping into little more than gesturing and clichéd name-calling to condemn particular types of managers and management environments. But, if managerialism is ultimately so undesirable how might it be displaced? The question remains a testing one.

Key Words:

Capitalism, Ideology, Modernism, Normative, Reification.

References

Anderson (2008); Clarke, Gerwitz and McLaughlin (2000); Hodge and Coronado (2006); Kuhn (2009); Mueller and Carter (2005).

Manipulation

Manipulation is the act of handling, steering or guiding events, situations or somebody's actions for one's own gain or interests. In terms of management and organization, manipulation occasionally arises where employees or **managers** seek to control or influence situations to their advantage through, for example, politicking (see **politics**) and bullying. This, in turn, may generate **resistance** to existing **structures** and **authority** by those who feel they are being manipulated.

Key Words:

Authority, Politics, Resistance, Structure.

References

Fay (2008); Parker (1997).

Marxism

The **politics** and philosophy of Marxism derive from the work of Karl Marx (1818–1883). Marx examined transformations in society, capitalism and industry and the embedded **power** relations taking place during the Industrial Revolution (see the entry on **capitalism** for a more expansive discussion). The impact and influence of Marx's writings has been monumental and enduring (Marx, 1867/1967).

Marxism cannot properly be described as a predominant or powerful influence on **Critical Management Studies** (CMS), however it has played an incipient role in the gestation and genesis of the sphere (see Fournier and Grey, 2000). A central recurrent theme within CMS, although not uncontested within critical accounts, is the aim of **emancipation** or at least micro-emancipation for research subjects and people in organizational roles (Alvesson and Willmott, 1996; Spicer, Alvesson and Kärreman, 2009). This goes hand in hand with a general anti-**capitalism**, anti-**commodification**, counter-**hegemonic** posture – all things kindred to Marxist discussion. The left-wing, socialist aspects, or even – at one end of the spectrum – revolutionary aspects of Marxism are evident as an undertone in CMS writings. This is to say that, while CMS is not Marxist, there are nevertheless shades of the ideological (see **ideology**) commitments of such movements and philosophies.

Key Words:

Capitalism, Critical Management Studies, Emancipation, Ideology, Industrial Revolution, Marxism, Politics, Power.

References

Alvesson and Willmott (1992, 1996); Fournier and Grey (2000); Marx (1867/1967); Peci (2009); Sewell (2005); Thomas and Davies (2005); Willmott (2005).

Masculinity (plural and field name: masculinities)

Masculinity, and the field of *masculinities*, concerns the study of the sociology, sexuality, role and behaviour of the male gender, condition and situation. It can be seen as something of a counterpart, although not a competitor field, to the role of feminism and womens' studies. The field of masculinity studies has been something of a subsequent development to feminism and, indeed, in relation to the overall debate on sexual roles and issues. It recognizes that the situation of the male gender in the contemporary era is a complex one and cannot be taken for granted.

Historically, the workplace was largely a male domain with men controlling the vast majority of roles especially with regard to managerial and directive posts. In line with this historical hegemonic (see **hegemony**) male position, differences and inequalities between feminine and masculine **genders** still exist in the modern workplace; however, women now hold a wider range of senior posts and pursue careers in more fields than was previously the case. This, of course, does not mean that challenges and impediments continue to exist for varying social groupings of both men and women.

Key Words:

Feminism, Gender, Sexuality.

References

Ball and Brewis (2008); Blomberg (2009); Bowring and Brewis (2009); Murgia and Poggio (2009).

McDonaldization

McDonalds is unquestionably among the world's most well-known brands. These fast food retail stores are famous for selling burger-style meals in a consistent formula that operates across all outlets. Although slight variations may exist in stores located in different countries, essentially, and almost irrespective of national context, McDonald's guarantees similar products, in similar-looking outlets, at relatively similar prices (adjusted for national cost of living) across the globe. The whole point of developing and using a homogenized, standardized and globalized process like this is to achieve a 'winning formula' where customers are guaranteed to know what they are getting for their money. Apparently it is what many consumers want – cheap food, served quickly with a particular contemporary experience or atmosphere associated with it. For McDonald's the commercial benefits are customer loyalty, efficient and effective supply and distribution chains leading to heightened economies of scale and thereby an opportunity to keep costs low and profits high.

The above situation might seem ideal in some ways but McDonaldization has been highly problematized in a number of respects. Ritzer's work, *The McDonaldization of Society* (1993), was the catalytic work for much of this critique. In his text, Ritzer expressed a series of concerns regarding the impacts of the rolling out and application of processes of dehumanized rational organization to wider areas of society, including schools, hospitals and public services (see **rationality**). As he saw it the McDonaldization of society overlooked integral and important human aspects that are part of our lives at work.

It is possible to see McDonaldization as an extension of, or allied to, other rational (see **rationality**) forms of mass organization and production, for example, **Taylorism** (centred on ideas of work measurement with the aim of improving task efficiency) and **Fordism** (concerned with large-scale fixed mass-production of homogenized products). All of these movements situate considerable **power** and control with management. As alluded to already, in keeping with these approaches to mass and standardized organization, McDonaldization is also charged with having little genuine regard for the social needs or well-being of workers. Indeed, it is frequently noted that McDonaldized environments often oblige employees to display particular attitudes and emotional responses to customers. A typical example of this is the cheery 'Have a nice day!'. This aspect of work is described as *emotional labour* (see **emotion**) and was powerfully commented on by Hochschild (1983) to portray the way in which, for example, air stewards and stewardesses have to remain charming and smile at passengers in all circumstances. Of course, this behaviour is an integral part of the McDonaldized 'service offering'. Consequently, there is a tendency sometimes to think of McDonaldization uniquely as a banal form of work organization. In fact, in order for McDonaldized processes to be able to achieve their aims, extensive (if not at times sinister and questionable) monitoring and **surveillance** of employees is frequently required. This ensures employees are compliant with prescribed standardized processes.

Is McDonaldization a good or a bad thing? It can be said that it is of course a good thing to be able to organize work efficiently and effectively and to achieve lower costs through the attainment of economies of scale (for example, bulk-buying of raw materials for relatively standardized products – buns for burgers). Few businesses would decline such an opportunity. But there are effects and problems as result of McDonaldizing things and people. Do McDonaldized environments truly respect people either as employees or as customers? It might be that both are merely units, or means to an end – a part of a larger rationalization for profit and corporate and market **power**. On a wider note, some commentators have made the reflexive turn and suggested that even Ritzer's book and thesis, the work which opened so much of the debate, is itself little more than a McDonaldized approach to the production of **knowledge** (see **reflexivity**). It has been proposed that books like Ritzer's (and, for comparison, Bryman's similar themed ideas on the **Disneyization** of society) fashionably commodify **knowledge** (see **commodification**) and opportunistically identify a 'branded' and logo-ed' theory rather than producing a debate more synthesized into wider academic knowledge and discussion. McDonaldization remains a powerful indicator or symbol (see **symbolism**) of the inevitability of standardization and homogenization implicit in processes of globalization.

Key Words:

Alienation, Disneyization, Emotional Labour, Fordism, Taylorism.

References

Bryman (2004); Dey and Steyaert (2007); Hochschild (1983); Kociatkiewicz and Kostera (2010); Ritzer (1993).

Meaning

The meaning of something concerns what humans understand and how they feel, react, interpret and make sense of it. The search for meaning is very much part of the social sciences (in contrast to the natural sciences which seek to understand and explain physical, chemical and biological processes and mechanisms). Meanings are not necessarily fixed and are likely to change over time. Also, meanings are commonly grounded in **language**, **discourse**, signs, **symbols** and myriad of other modes and means. For example, it is common for people to employ **stories**, **metaphors** and **narratives** in order to explore and elaborate their significance, meanings and implications. Human beings constantly need to consider various degrees and dimensions of meaning in the events and processes of their own lives and those of others. In particular, there is often a felt need for meaning in times of adversity through which people need to find a way forward.

The search for meaning is an important quest in a wide range of social science research and organization and management is no exception. Attempts at identifying 'meaning' employ a variety of epistemological and ontological **paradigms** and approaches (see **epistemology** and **ontology**). **Critical Management Studies** (CMS) has a tendency to lean towards interpretive, subjective, constructivist and relativistic **sense-making** approaches in developing meaning (see **interpretivism**, **subjectivity** and **social constructivism**).

Key Words:

Discourse, Language, Narrative, Paradigm, Sense-making, Stories, Subjectivity.

References

Corona and Godart (2010); De Clerq and Voronov (2009); Fairhurst (2004); Martens (2006).

Meta-narrative

Meta is the Greek work for 'above' or 'over' and therefore the term 'meta-narrative' means an all-encompassing **narrative**, account or **story**. Given the **hegemony of modernistic** and **positivistic paradigms** (see **modernism** and **positivism**) of the nineteenth and early twentieth centuries, a wide range of meta-narratives have emerged across the arts and sciences building on earlier work. To some greater or lesser extent, examples of **theory**-building in this vein could be said to include, for example, Darwin's (1809–1882) work the *Origin of Species*, Newton's (1643–1727) work in physics and mathematics and Descartes (1596–1650) studies in relation to philosophy and rationalism see **rationality**. A critique of the meta-narrative forms of these accounts, along with a general critique of **modernism**, was brought to prominence by the French philosopher Jean-Francois Lyotard (1924–1988) in his 1984 publication: *The Postmodern Condition: A Report on Knowledge* in which he elaborated that the **emergence** of science and scientific **knowledge** had been a key hegemonic meta-narrative of the twentieth century (see **hegemony**).

Critical Management Studies (CMS) approaches take issue with the use of meta-narratives to provide all-encompassing accounts of phenomena and the reductionist and over-delineated manner that characterizes them (see **reductionism** and **linearity**). In other words, for

CMS, meta-narratives are too generalized and tend to overlook a significant degree of variation and subjective diversity (see **subjectivity**) in situations and contexts. Equally, given their modernistic origins, meta-narratives tend to suggest the appearance of things being fixed and unchanging. Again, CMS takes issue with this suggesting that a more meaningful version of managerial and organizational spheres is provided through accounts that subscribe to a more evolving set of images and micro-narratives (i.e. smaller scale, localized **narratives** and **stories**) rather than meta-narratives.

Key Words:

Discourse, Emergence, Hegemonic, Modernism, Narrative, Positivism, Story.

References

Boje (2008); Caldwell (2007); Gabriel (2000); Lyotard (1979); Thomas and Davies (2005).

Metaphor

A metaphor is a form of comparison between two events or objects. An intention of this comparison is to create vivid and poignant images and understanding for an audience. A simple literary example of a metaphor might be, 'the farmer's tractor sailed across the waves of the ploughed field'. The 'field' in literal terms is clearly not a 'sea' nor the tractor a 'ship' but the analogy to these images is made in order to provide a vibrant impression of the style and tenor of the scene in the recipient's mind. Metaphors are a prominent feature in many literatures and across a span of disciplines.

Metaphors are used extensively in everyday life of which, of course, organizational life plays an integral part. Metaphors are often incorporated into **story** and **narrative** structures and they are used as a device employed across **normative/mainstream** and critical perspective approaches. A seminal organizational text in developing thinking in relation to metaphors was Gareth Morgan's (1997) *Images of Organization* which discussed the underlying metaphorical foundations in organization and management.

Key Words:

Narrative, Story.

References

Gabriel (2005); Kavanagh (2009); Morgan (1997); Mutch (2005).

Mimesis (adjective: mimetic)

The Concise Oxford English Dictionary indicates 'mimesis' as a term nominally associated within the field of biology:

> A close external resemblance of an animal to another that is distasteful or harmful to predators of the first.

'Mimesis' is derived from the Greek work *mimetikos* meaning 'imitation' and, in organizational terms, pertains to replicating, imitating and copying behaviour by organizations. In organization and management there are, and continue to be, many fads and fashions of latest thinking, techniques on organizational processes, strategies and structures (Newell, Robertson and Swan, 2001). The potential list is long but illustrations of these might include, for example, coaching, benchmarking, total quality management, business process re-engineering, best practice and lean manufacturing. The assumption underlying the adoption and implementation by senior managers of new techniques and approaches is that they will provide organizations with enhanced competitive advantage to differentiate them from their competitors or, at the very least, to ensure that they keep up with them. In the spirit of the biological definition, acquiring competitive attributes and appearances may also dissuade competitors (that is to say, predators) from attacking or encroaching on a firm's space or territory. Thereby, organizations aim to make themselves less susceptible to 'attack'. An important point to note here is that such copying is predicated on the assumption that particular fads and fashions are 'believed to be' successful. In fact, the effects of such approaches or initiatives may not be particularly tried or tested and may well turn out to have significant downsides in the longer run. Therefore, being seen to adopt or implement a new approach is often as much a political or cultural gesture by managers and organizations in a form of 'keeping up with the Jones' and through a fear of being left behind (see **politics** and **culture**). From a **Critical Management Studies** (CMS) perspective the notion that there is 'one best way' or a right way or single answer to an organization is unacceptable and alien. Critical accounts tend to view mimetic processes as, frequently, problematic and more a consequence of **hegemonic modernistic** political and socio-cultural pressures (Newell, Robertson and Swan, 2001; Atkin, Hassard and Wolfram Cox, 2007; Rhodes and Westwood, 2008) (see **hegemony**, **modernism**, **politics** and **culture**).

Key Words:

Copying, Culture, Fashion, Hegemony, Imitation, Modernism, Politics.

References

Atkin, Hassard and Wolfram Cox (2007); Newell, Robertson and Swan (2001); Phillips and Rippin (2010); Rhodes and Westwood (2008).

Modernism (also modernity)

Modernism is a philosophy that prizes rationalism (see **rationality**). In so doing it tends to value **linearity** and numerical measurement to gauge, monitor and control its application. A central ideological commitment and engagement of modernism is the achievement of 'progress' through the (industrial) application of *science and scientific techniques* (see **ideology**). The presence of modernism in business and organizations can be witnessed as privileging (see **privilege**) objectified quantification of task and people (see **objectivity**). Examples of such measures include, for example, *staff turnover ratios, key performance indicators* (KPIs), *categorization of assets and liabilities, measurement of market share, share price and cash-flow projections.* In modernistic and managerialist (see **managerialism**) accounts of organizations it is anticipated that these indicators will supposedly reveal all that is imagined to be essential for running an effective and efficient organization. Clearly, these are indeed potentially useful measures for guiding the organization to corporate success but they are also prone to overlooking sociological, cultural and political issues and perspectives (see **cultural** and **political**). It also means that modernistic perspectives are prone to offering somewhat impersonal and dehumanized **representations** of organizational life.

In the broadest sense, beyond organization and management commentaries, 'modernity' is a term that also refers to approximate historical period(s) in which modernism and modernistic approaches and philosophies are deemed to have emerged and been potently influential. From a social science and **Critical Management Studies** (CMS) viewpoint modernism is also viewed as a largely hegemonic influence (**hegemony**).

It is difficult to locate the precise moment when the period(s) termed 'modernity' commenced but its roots are frequently suggested to be situated in **The Enlightenment** of the seventeenth and eighteenth centuries. A wide range of writers contributed to this tradition and, in particular, the French philosopher Rene Descartes (1713–1784) developed a range of thought based on rationalism (see **rationality**). Descartes was interested in examining the mind and body as distinct and separate entities and the potential consequences of this (see **dualism**). Subsequent writers such as Voltaire (1694–1778), Rousseau (1712–1778) and Diderot (1713–1784) elaborated ideas on related themes as did British writers such as Adam Smith (1723–1790), David Hume (1711–1776) and Sir Issac Newton (1643–1727). In large part, commentators such as these were keen to explore and challenge prevailing hegemonic patterns of thinking that were sourced and sponsored by long-standing religious, aristocratic hierarchical **structures**, superstitions or traditional beliefs (see **hegemony**, **hierarchy**, **normative**, **mainstream**). One of the principle means of modernistic developments was through the use of the emerging fields and alternative perspectives offered by *science and scientific method*. Science very quickly became espoused with the notion of progress for the human condition and society as a whole. This in turn, it was postulated, would assist in producing changes in social conditions leading to rights, natural justice and **emancipation** for individuals and society from existing constraints and limitations.

Modernism as a commanding pattern of thinking in the Western world is generally considered to have been at its most potent and widespread in the late nineteenth and early twentieth centuries. Hand in hand with the emergence of modernism and the growing influence of rationalism (see **rationality**), the Industrial Revolution unfolded in Europe. Many of the ideas and principles of scientific and rationalistic thought were symbiotically responsible for, and/or applied to, the developments that were taking place in wider society: a heightened organization of industrial rather than agrarian production; organization of work into specialized trades and tasks within factories – the division of labour and specialization of task; creation of new towns in place of rural and agrarian cottage or craft-based societies; and, the application of science to new industrial processes and the development of technologies and machines to increase efficiency and attain mass-production. Within these 'new worlds' the role of the **manager** came into being and developed.

'Modernism' has become the generic term that **represents** the manner in which this rationalistic ideology was applied to a range of fields (see **ideology**). In tandem with industrial activity, modernism infused a wide range of societal activities. It emerged as an artistic style offering depersonalized, clean constructions and objectivized, linear representations of its subjects in architecture, poetry, writing and painting (see **objectivity**, **linearity** and **representation**). In these respective fields, important exponents include: *inter alia* Le Corbusier (1887–1965), Joyce (1882–1941), Kandinsky (1866–1944) and Duchamps (1887–1968). All of these fused modernistic principles, scientific and technological approaches and appreciations into their work (Dereli and Stokes, 2007).

There is no doubt that, in the contemporary era, the legacy and practice of modernism continues to shape organizations and exert influence. The momentum of the *modernist project* is such that it was seen to become all-encompassing and **hegemonic**, dominating and eclipsing of other philosophies and approaches (see **hegemony**). Lyotard (1979) described this as the dominant **meta-narrative** (a **narrative** or **story** embracing all aspects of micro and macro and all domains) of the twentieth century.

A significant negative consequence of modernism, however, is the potential dehumanization and marginalization of the human condition. In the context of large factories, managerialist control (see **managerialism**), mass-production, mass-markets, mass-consumption present issues and difficulties for individual **identity**. It was quickly recognized by observers and commentators that modernism, modernity and the associated industrialization and science it employed often subjugated and oppressed human beings in the social, living and working arrangements it engendered. It also created new **power** elites to replace those who had dominated in premodernity (see **premodernism**). This was particularly pointed at by Marx (see **Marxism**) on **capitalism** and exponents of **Critical Theory** such as Horkheimer (1895–1973), Adorno (1903–1969) and Marcuse (1898–1979). Moreover, significantly, the objectivizing and alienating tendencies of modernism have been argued as leading to stark situations (see **objectivity** and **alienation**). Bauman, in his 1989 work, *Modernity and the Holocaust*, demonstrates how the horror of the Nazi Holocaust was not an aberration of, and departure from, 'normal' or **normative** society but rather was an inevitable consequence of the modernistic and bureaucratic **structures**, machinery, approaches and behaviours which, by the mid-twentieth century, had become so embedded and automatic in society (see **bureaucracy**).

Many contemporary accounts of business management and organizations continue to be premised on modernistic assumptions resulting in discussions and actions that are seemingly logical, rationale and objective (see **rationality** and **objectivity**). At the same time, they may equally be less effective at taking account of more 'messy problems', complexity and those aspects of organizations where **subjectivity** and a range of varying and contrasting perceptions and understanding may exist simultaneously (Eden, 1987). Such complexities are very much part of the human condition and it is often the simplistic representations of human motive, behaviour and action which modernistic accounts potentially gloss over because they do not fit with a normative or mainstream set of preoccupations, myopias and obsessions. CMS accounts of management and organizations contrast considerably with modernistic renditions. CMS, with its embrace of a range of relativistic, subjective philosophical stances often challenges and confronts modernism and its ideological commitments (see **subjectivity** and **ideology**).

Key Words:

Hegemony, Linearity, Objectivity, Rationality, Science, Scientific Method, Subjectivity.

References

Dereli and Stokes (2007); Eden (1987); Lyotard (1979); Peci (2009); Townley (2002).

Morality

Morality is concerned with the goodness or badness of human behaviour. It includes notions concerning the rules that aim to regulate or govern that behaviour and assist in determining 'right' and 'wrong'. If a person is seen as behaving in a way generally considered to be 'good' or appropriate we may call them a 'moral person'. If the opposite occurs we may call the person, or his or her actions, immoral. If, however, a person is so without any sense of morality or boundaries to their conduct they may well be described as amoral (i.e. devoid or without any sense of morality) (see **boundary**). Morality is closely aligned with **ethics**. *Normative ethics* are concerned with attempts to make clear decisions and distinctions between what is good or bad. On the other hand, the area of *descriptive ethics* seeks to analyse and portray what ethical choices might be encompassed in a given situation.

If society or a community has aspirations to operate in a civilized or harmonious manner, then morality is generally considered to be a very important consideration. For people working in organizations and management this is equally valid. Recent examples of issues provoking debates around morality and **ethics** in a United Kingdom context include bankers' bonuses, salary and pay-offs for top executives and Member of Parliament expenses to name but a few.

In business school curricula, the area of morality is more often than not seen as being addressed in modules on 'Business Ethics' and 'Corporate Governance'. While a number of insights are generated by such modules, it is often argued that they tend to be couched in **normative** ethics and **mainstream** modernistic and positivistic assumptions and ideologies (see **modernism**, **positivism** and **ideology**). This means that although it is understood that the vast majority of **managers** and employees may not wish to do anything immoral or unethical, this may not always be so straightforward. Given the many demands and pressures to which employees are subjected, ultimately the dictates of effectiveness, efficiency, profits and **performativity** may overrule what would generally be considered appropriate or 'right' judgement. In contrast, critical approaches to morality and ethics tend to follow a model more affiliated to the descriptive ethical model. Critical commentaries are interested in pointing at the multiple interpretations, constructions and perspectives that may be at play in a given context or setting.

Key Words:

Amoral, Bad, Boundary, Ethics, Good, Ideology, Immoral, Mainstream, Modernism, Normative, Performativity, Positivism.

References

Jensen, Sandström and Helin (2009); Stokes and Gabriel (2010).

Myth

A myth can be considered as a traditional **narrative** or **story** that mixes fact and fiction and whose complete factual truthfulness is difficult to determine. Often myths may include elements of superstition or fantasy. A myth therefore can be seen as a tale often believed but in many ways founded in fiction. Myths do not exist uniquely in relation to ancient times or **premodernism**. They have been very much a part of human history in all eras and no less so in the contemporary period. Myths operate and reign in many workplaces regarding the apparent exploits or events or people. They can be significant ways to convey or develop **meaning** among groups of people.

Employing the term 'myth' can also be an act of denigration or dismissiveness. To say that something is a myth in the oft-heard phrase 'it's just a myth' frequently represents a strong suggestion that it is widely talked about as having some **truth** or validity but it does not, in fact, have any truth at all (see **representation**).

Key Words:

Meaning, Narrative, Premodernism, Story, Truth.

References

Gabriel (2000, 2004); Hjorth and Pelzer (2007).

Nn

Narrative

Narrative consists of a series of events, a **discourse** or incidents which are related in some form of order to convey particular **meanings**, impressions and understandings to an audience. Narratives are often spoken or written but equally they may be conveyed through images or **symbols**. The term '**narratives**' is often used interchangeably with the term **stories**. However, it should be noted that distinctions and definitions between thcsc terms are not always clear-cut. There is a long-standing engagement with narratives across a number of disciplines. Literature embracing novels, plays, prose, poetry and theatre naturally engages with issues surrounding narrative. The *history discipline* also has been an area where debates on narratives have been developed (Ricouer, 1984).

Lyotard (1979) suggested that modernity and the twentieth century had been represented primarily by a series of *grand* narratives, or dominant **hegemonic meta-narratives**, that embodied politics, ideology (particularly in relation to the **Cold War**), **culture** and religion (see **modernism, representation** and **politics**). In the contemporary period it has become commonplace to suggest that more fragmented, individual and localized micro-narratives have become increasingly prevalent as a pattern of sense-making and understanding. Narratives are often viewed as allowing the author to better portray the **lived experience** of situations and events – they evoke vitality and a sense of genuinely feeling or sensing the context under examination. Overall, narratives and **stories** have now become a popular and widely employed approach within organization and management studies (Polkinghorne, 1988; Czarniawska, 1998, 2004; Gabriel, 2000). They afford opportunities to discuss and understand the ways in which individuals and groups engage in: **sense-making**, **social constructionism**, negotiate, build and transform identities (see **identity**) in organizational, management and life settings.

Key Words:

Discourse, *Grand Narrative*, Meta-Narrative, Modernism, Representation, Stories.

References

Czarniawska (1998, 2004); Essers (2009); Gabriel (2000); Lyotard (1979); Polkinghorne (1988); Rhodes and Brown (2005); Ricouer (1984).

Normative

The notion of normative involves laying down rules or guidelines. Normative is very much about what people *should* do in a given situation. It is also about suggesting actions that would be considered appropriate in arriving at optimum or ideal solutions and is influenced by social norms, expectations and the context in which a given action or behaviour is taking place. For example, a person is more likely to be relaxed with close office work colleagues or friends than in a boardroom or in a meeting with an important client. In other words, these differing instances carry normative expectations regarding employee behaviour.

Critical Management Studies (CMS) generally critiques and investigates normative and **mainstream** approaches to organization and management. CMS typically identifies and comments on their **Enlightenment** – influenced, modernistic, objectified, representationalist, managerialist propositions and stances on management and organizational issues (see **modernism**, **objectivity**, **representation** and **managerialism**). In place of these, CMS tends to suggest a range of philosophical approaches (for example, among others, **postmodernism**, **poststructuralism**, and **Critical Theory**) that explore the **subjectivity**, relativistic and constructionist ways of understanding organization and management (see **social constructionism**). The **dialectic** between critical approaches and **normative** approaches is often not stated explicitly in critical texts but constitutes a recurrent subtext. Reciprocally, it is not uncommon for **normative**-style approaches to pay little or no regard to the concerns that preoccupy critical viewpoints (for example, the subjectivities (see **subjectivity**) and relativities of **power**, **discourse**, **knowledge**, **boundary**, **identity** and so on and so forth.

Key Words:

Critical Theory, Enlightenment, Managerialism, Modernism, Objectivity, Postmodernism, Poststructuralism, Representation, Social Constructionism, Subjectivity.

References

Blomberg (2009); Kavanagh (2009); Murgia and Poggio (2009).

Objectivity

Something is considered objective when it is seen to be free and independent from particular feelings, opinions, **emotions** or sentiments. When someone or something displays these characteristics he, she or it is said to show *objectivity*. Objectivity is a central plank of the scientific approach to building **knowledge** (see **epistemology**) and an important principle of **positivism** and **modernism**. For adherents of objectivized approaches, knowledge thus created is said to contain **truth** and validity. An important concept within this view of objectivity is that such truths exist independent of, and external to, the mind and body of the observer or researcher. They have an ontological solidity (see **ontology**).

Modernism and **positivism** have for large parts of the twentieth and twenty-first centuries been **hegemonic** influences on the shape and development of management and organization theory and practice. A central construct of this has been the espousal of a particular view of objectivity, **rationality** and **linearity**. This has tended to exclude or marginalize alternative philosophical, **political** and sociological perspectives such as those embraced by **Critical Management Studies** (CMS). It is a complex issue, but in general, critical approaches tend to embrace **subjectivity** and, rather than prizing objectivity, tend to problematize it suggesting that it overlooks many ways of how **sense-making** and **meaning** may take place in organizational life.

Key Words:

Emotion, Epistemology, Hegemonic, Linearity, Meaning, Modernism, Sense-making, Subjectivity, Truth.

References

Golsorkhi, Leca, Lounsbury and Ramirez (2009); Willmott (2009).

Ontology (adjective: ontological)

Ontology is about individuals' attitudes towards perceptions of *reality*. It is not uncommon in everyday life for many people to simply take **reality** unquestioningly. This is rooted in objectivism (see **objectivity**) which believes that objects and issues exist *outside* the observer and independent to any role that he or she has in relation to perceiving or sensing them. This is the positivistic position broadly adopted by **normative**, **mainstream**, modernistic and managerialist (see **modernism** and **managerialism**) approaches to researching management and organization (see **positivism**).

Ontology is equally concerned with questions about what is the substance of existence or being – in other words, what do we believe about the solidity or concreteness of reality? Various philosophical perspectives have differing ideas about the ontological basis of their approach. For example, **positivism** adopts what might be termed a *naïve realism*. This is a term **meaning** that reality is taken at face value. Alternatively, for example, **critical realism**, **postmodernism** and **poststructuralism**, in their own ways, and to differing degrees, argue for more subjectively (see **subjectivity**) informed approaches in developing an understanding of the ontological nature of things.

However, it is possible to challenge this **objectivist** point of view. Such challenges can be centred on a subjectivist (see **subjectivity**) perspective of **reality**. This suggests that while it might be the case that people witness external objects, events and issues, nevertheless, the sense that they make or construct of them may vary depending on individual and contextual factors (see **sense-making** and **social construction**). In other words, the **meaning** of a given perceived reality is very much dependent on the person(s) forming that perception and to some extent it might be felt that 'the **truth** is in the eye of the beholder'. Overall, critical perspective approaches tend to be more aligned with subjectivist style ontologies.

Key Words:

Being, Existence, Mainstream, Meaning, Normative, Objectivity, Positivism, Relativism, Social Construction, Solidity, Subjectivity.

References

Bryman and Bell (2007); Fleetwood (2005); Jankowicz (2005); Linstead and Brewis (2007).

Organization

It is possible to think of 'organization' as a way of going about tasks, taking actions or arranging and ordering things. It might be argued that there is a propensity for human beings to organize to some greater or lesser degree rather than choose to live with disorder or chaos. Organizing can therefore be considered as attempts to establish **structures** and systems for particular social, political and cultural (see **politics** and **culture**) purposes. This embraces structuring the shape of a company or process and the work of people.

Organization and management is not something that should be thought of as beginning in, or emerging, uniquely as a consequence of the Industrial Revolution. The introduction of **structure**, order, routine, patterns into human activities and affairs is something that has taken place since earliest times. What the Industrial Revolution did indeed achieve was striking *alternative and novel* forms of organizing. *Organization **Theory*** is a body of **knowledge** that develops and analyses the thinking and commentary on organization. These domains embrace issues of *organizational **politics***, *organizational **identity*** (the distinctive image or presence of a given organization), *organizational **culture*** (a particular internal atmosphere and environment), *organizational learning* and so on and so forth. In **normative** or conventional organizational **theory** there is a tendency for organizational analysis to examine the environment and the objectives of the firm and to undertake a process whereby an organizational structure and form is adopted, from the range of forms available, which seems most suited to the achievement of the objectives in the given environment. This gives the impression of a rational and logical process at work; however, it belies the role of a wide range of power, political effects and subjective relations and perspectives which are likely to emerge during the process (see **impression management**; **rationality**, **politics**, **subjectivity** and **emergence**).

In contrast to **normative** and **mainstream** approaches, **Critical Management Studies** (CMS) embraces a range of perspectives in regard to examining organizations including, for example, **Critical Realism**, **Deconstructionism**, **Feminism**, **Postmodernism**, **Post-structuralism** (there are many more possible domains). Each philosophical approach brings its own ideological (see **ideology**) commitments and beliefs to bear onto organizations. CMS has focused considerable energy on analysing and dissecting extant organization **theory** and organizational forms. In particular, it has been eager to discuss the **experience** of organizations as fluid, organic, rhizomatic and ever-changing rather than stable and fixed (see **rhizome**). CMS perspectives have taken great interest in exploring issues of **resistance**, identity, **power**, sexuality, speed, excess, **discourse**, **gender**, **aesthetics**, **sense-making**, **surveillance**, **stories and narrative**, oppression, among many others, in relation to organizations and the people who work in and around them (Adler, 2009; Alvesson and Billing, 2009; Alvesson, Bridgeman and Willmott, 2009; Boje, 2008; Bolton and Houlihan, 2009; Carter and Jackson, 2006; Clegg, Kornberger and Pitsis, 2008; Fineman, Gabriel and Sims, 2009; Gabriel, 2000; Grey, 2008; Gustafson, Rehn and Skold, 2005; Jones and Ten Bos, 2007; Listead, Fulop and Lilley, 2009).

Key Words:

Aesthetics, Discourse, Excess, Flexible, Gender, Identity, Mainstream, Narrative, Normative, Oppression, Power, Resistance, Sense-making, Stories, Surveillance.

References

Adler (2009); Alvesson and Billing (2009); Alvesson, Bridgeman and Willmott (2009); Boje (2008); Bolton and Houlihan (2009); Carter and Jackson (2006); Clegg, Kornberger and Pitsis (2008); Fineman, Gabriel and Sims (2010); Gabriel (2000); Grey (2008); Gustafson, Rehn and Skold (2005); Jones and Ten Bos (2007); Linstead, Fulop and Lilley (2009); Linstead and Linstead (2005).

Other

'Other' is a term used in philosophy in a sense somewhat, but not completely, removed from its everyday sense. The act and **experience** of 'othering' plays a significant role in contemporary philosophical, **gender** and **postcolonial discourses**. In philosophical discussion it points at the processes whereby, through, **discourse** and **representation**, a particular **identity** or set of characteristics is produced for, and transposed onto, another person, group or object. This is a process termed as 'othering'. This can often have the effect of diminishing a person's sense of feeling human and their overall sense of integral **identity**. 'Othering' pathologizes and casts out the person, rendering him or her 'untouchable' and dehumanized. Othering is an act that employs **power** and removes or **silences** the **voices** of those 'othered'. In organizational terms these are often talked about as part of process of bullying and harassment.

In a management and organization context, othering can take place between, for example, employees or between, say, a manager and an employee. This can result in the gradual removal of the 'shared' human characteristics and empathy from the rest of the group, team or organization. In other words, he or she becomes separate and compassion for the 'othered' person's plight fades. As the extreme end of a process of 'othering' it may be possible for the 'othered' person to be cast aside, for example, redundancy, dismissal or long-term illness. In the worst circumstances, as a consequence of othering, a person might suffer a fatal illness such as a breakdown, stroke or heart attack.

Key Words:

Bullying, Discourse, Harassment, Humanism, Othering, Pathologization, Power, Representation, Silence.

References

Czarniawska and Hopfl (2002); Hearn (1996); Law and Singleton (2005); Stokes and Gabriel (2010); Woźniak (2010).

Pp

Panopticon

The panopticon came to prominence through the English philosopher Jeremy Bentham (1748–1832). In the physical sense, the panopticon consists of a design for a cylindrical building structure. Around the outer edge walls of the cylinder are individual cells, rooms or spaces. In the centre is located an observation tower with windows on all sides with the capability of viewing all the cells. The overall structure would allow an observer or overseer to potentially watch every cell almost simultaneously or at least very readily.

The model is a theoretical one but has nevertheless been discussed within **Critical Management Studies** (CMS) as a type of mechanism and structure that illustrates **surveillance** in operation. Those working or based in the panopticon do not realize when or why they are being watched. Potentially, they could be under **surveillance** at any give moment. Because individuals have this uncertainty it reproduces (see **reproduction**) the effect that people begin to even censure, 'police' or monitor their own actions – just in case they are being watched.

With the expansion of the use of CCTV camera networks in work and public spaces, together with workplace email monitoring, it can be envisaged how the principle portrayed by Bentham's panopticon plays out in the electronic contemporary era. The French philosopher Michel Foucault (1926–1984) in his work **Discipline** and Punish: The Birth of the Prison (1975/1979) discusses how the impact of surveillance, auto-surveillance (individuals monitoring and controlling themselves for fear they may be being watched at any given moment), linked to issues of **power** and **authority**, operates in society. Equally, in wider litera-ture this image is captured poignantly in George Orwell's novel *Nineteen Eighty-Four* which portrays the novel's protagonist, Winston, wrestling with an internal struggle forcing him to comply with the dictates and propaganda of the totalitarian governing party and yet, simultaneously, trying to escape the omnipresent eyes and surveillance of the hegemonic ruling elite (see **hegemony**). In summary, within critical texts, the term 'panopticon' (or the adjective *panoptic*) generally works as a byword associated with issues of control and surveillance that produce and reproduce **power**, oppression, **authority** and disempowerment.

Key Words:

Discipline, Oppression, Power, Reproduction, Resistance, Surveillance.

References

Caldwell (2007); Fleming (2001 – *a book review contextualising issues relating to the panopticon*); Foucault (1975/1979); Gabriel (2005); Robertson (2003); Townley (2005).

Paradigm

A paradigm comprises a model underpinned by particular beliefs and val-ues. Adherence and commitment to a given model can, in turn, lead to consequent actions by individuals, groups and **organizations**. In other words, a paradigm is, in effect, a **representation** of a belief *system*, embracing values, concepts, ideas and assumptions that guide a person's actions in relation to either a specific subject and/or potentially wider events in his or her life. Drawing on popular examples, it might be possi-ble to consider something like *New Labour*, *Marxism* or *Environmentalism* as paradigms of one form or another. Moreover, it is possible to suggest that, through the explicit development of particular corporate **cultures**, a company or **organization** grows and nurtures a particular **sense-making** paradigm for the people who are employed by, and interact with it (see Johnson, Scholes and Whittington, 2008).

In relation to the conduct of research, academics and researchers will frequently explicitly align themselves with a particular paradigm and this will influence how they approach, conduct and produce research findings (Watson, 2006). Strong belief in, and adherence to, particular paradigms has often created tensions and powerful disagreements between differ-ing academic communities. Perhaps most prominent of these are the debates between natural scientific methodological approaches and social scientific approaches (see Lincoln and Guba, 1985; Denzin and Lincoln, 2008). Scientific approaches are notionally founded on claims that follow the establishment of a **hypothesis** or **hypotheses**. They follow pre-set processes in order to gather notionally objective data with a view to proving or disproving the **hypotheses** (see **objectivity**). On the other hand, social science approaches frequently adopt methodological approaches, and paradigms, that aim to acknowledge the role of **subjectivity** in trying to understand situations. Many social scientists find it improbable that research can be completely objective (see **objectivity**) – there will always be some human subjective judgement and choice at play. Social science approaches believe that if this is not taken into account in a holistic way then we oversimplify or lose some of the richness of possible understanding.

In the light of the differences between natural and social science methods and commentators, heated exchanges might be expected. For example, Kuhn (1970) generated considerable controversy by pointing at the way that peer relationships and **politics** in scientific communities play a **subjective** role in determining what becomes and what does not become 'established science'. In a counter charge, natural scientists often find that the claims of social scientists are too **subjective** and too dependent on data that cannot be verified in a way they believe is repeatable and objective.

Within organization and management studies, Burrell and Morgan (1979) attempted to argue and chart organizational and management research paradigms diagrammatically using an axis of:

- **objectivity** (the organization is seen as real and we look at it as an external observer)
- **subjectivity** (the organization is the result of human interaction and **social construction** – a result of the multiple everyday long-term events and exchanges that create the place where people work)

interfaced on the opposing axis with:

- **regulatory** (the role of research is to describe what happens in organizations)
- **radical** (the role of research is to prescribe what should happen in organizations)

Trying to classify paradigms in this way provides a potentially useful aid and may help to develop understanding how the various paradigms situate or position ideologically in relation to one and another. However, this type of categorization has also been criticized for attempting to draw boundaries between the different characteristics of different paradigms when in fact it is not always so delineated or straightforward (see **boundary** and **linear**).

Debates on paradigmatic positions have been central to the ongoing commentary in **Critical Management Studies** (CMS). A common approach in CMS critiques of management and organizations has been to target, for example, positivistic, managerialist and **normative representations of** organizations (see **positivism** and **managerialism**). These paradigms and **representations** are frequently grounded on the linear, objective and reductionist beliefs of a natural scientific approach to research and understanding the world (see **linearity, objectivity** and **reductionism**). In relation to the scientific-style approach to research, CMS is eager to show that such **representations** include the presence of **hegemonic**, unequal (i.e. asymmetrical) and oppressive **power** relations between various groups, **institutions** and **organizations**. In addressing these issues, CMS writings embrace a range of philosophical paradigms including, by way of illustration, **postmodernism**, **poststructuralism**, **deconstruction**, **social constructionism**, **feminism** and post-feminism. Furthermore, CMS argues that by analysing organizations through these alternative frames of reference a richer, more holistic and indeed humanistic understanding of organizational life and management can be developed. Such analyses are mindful of, for instance, the subjective, discursive, **power**, sexuality and emotional aspects of issues (**subjectivity**, **discourse** and **emotion**). However, as should be expected, the paradigmatic assumptions on which CMS constructs its arguments are not without their critics (see Thompson, 1993; Willmott, 2006, 2008; Cooke, 2008; Stookey, 2008). In this vein, issues surrounding the usefulness, **performativity** and transferability of CMS studies to actual organizational life have become topic of an important debate within the field (for an elaboration of this, please refer to the *Introduction*).

Key Words:

Beliefs, Ideology, Models, Perspectives, Values.

References

Burrell and Morgan (1979); Cooke (2008); Denzin and Lincoln (2008); Johnson, Scholes and Whittington (2008); Kuhn (1970); Lincoln and Guba (1985); Stookey (2008); Thompson (1993); Watson (2006); Willmott (2006, 2008).

Participant observation

Participant observation is a research method that involves gathering data by watching and studying people in a given setting or settings. Researchers using participant observation are keen to learn about, among other things, the patterns, **rituals**, **language**, **discourse**, **symbols** and signs that individuals and groups employ in order to make sense (see **sense-making**) and develop and convey **meaning** in their lives and interactions. Waddington (2004) provides a very useful overview of the participant observation in which he outlines a spectrum of participant observation approaches ranging from, at one end, *complete observation* (where the researcher deliberately attempts to be separate from the group and environment he or she is observing) to, at the other end of the spectrum, *complete participant*, wherein the researcher conducting participant observation is comprehensively implanted and integrated into the social group being observed – he or she takes part in everything that individuals and the overall group undertake. In many regards this latter situation provides the researcher with some sense of **lived experience** of the group.

Participant observation is part of an array of methods and approaches (that could include for example unstructured or semi-structured interviews) and often forms part of an interpretivistic, ethnographic approach (see **interpretivism, ethnography**). Indeed, the use of ethnographic approaches is very prevalent in **Critical Management Studies** (CMS) research. Furthermore, the notion of **reflexivity** plays an important role in participant observation research. This means that in observing people, it is significant to be mindful of the reciprocal interaction and exchanges between the researcher and the researched (i.e. the research subjects or respondents). In other words, the researcher plays a potentially important role in building up and influencing the research picture (see Wray-Bliss, 2004 and Wray-Bliss and Brewis 2008 on this issue).

Key Words:

Ethnography, Interpretivism, Lived Experience, Meaning, Reflexivity, Sense-making.

References

Allard-Poesi (2005); Badham, Garrety, Morrigan and Zanko (2003); Bryman and Bell (2007); Waddington (2004); Wray-Bliss (2004); Wray-Bliss and Brewis (2008).

Performativity

'Performativity' is a term used in both **normative/mainstream** and **Critical Management Studies** (CMS). For **normative** and **mainstream**-style commentaries, performativity concerns attempts to develop and improve efficiency and effectiveness in organizations. In many regards this is seen as a central responsibility of **managers**, through the use of techniques such as **empowerment**, teamwork and quality initiatives (such as total quality management and T-circles). Through leadership, managers should also encourage everyone to engage with this project. In the **normative** mould, performativity is underpinned by objective (see **objectivity**) numerical metrics such as profit, turnover, wastage figures, labour turnover, market share and so on and so forth.

Within **normative** approaches, performativity is embraced and discussed as a necessary, positive, and essentially unproblematized, concept aimed at improving the **organization**. In contrast, within CMS texts, the term 'performativity' has tended to be engaged with in a questioning, or even, pejorative sense. CMS texts are doubtful about the way in which **normative** and **mainstream** works talk about performativity as if it were readily and easily explained by reference to apparent objective measures such as statistics, accounting metrics or key performance indicators (see **objectivity**). CMS is eager to use, for example, ethnographic-style and critical realist accounts to portray the subjective, socially constructed and **lived experience** aspects of living and working with and around organizations (see **ethnography**, **Critical Realism**, **subjectivity** and **social constructionism**). More recently, with the growing maturity of CMS as a field, there have been moves to develop a more complex and sophisticated response to the issues of performativity. For example, Spicer, Alvesson and Kärreman (2009) have proposed that CMS is, in fact, very much a project concerned with performativity and that its purpose should be centred on attempts to develop 'progressive' forms of management and **organization.** They suggest that this can be further developed by:

> CMS becoming affirmative, caring, pragmatic, potential focused, and normative ... [by employing] ... a range of tactics including affirming ambiguity, working with mysteries, applied communicative action, exploring heterotopias and engaging micro-emancipations.
>
> (not in the original text – see **emancipatory** and **utopia**)

Key Words:

Lived Experience, Mainstream, Normative, Objectivity, Social Constructionism, Subjectivity.

References

Hodgson (2005); Keenoy and Seijo (2010); Spicer, Alvesson and Kärreman (2009).

Pluralism

Pluralism is the idea that there are many authentic and legitimate **paradigms**, views or **voices** that operate in an **organization** or institution. Pluralism contrasts with, for example, **unitary** views on organizations which anticipate that there will be one overriding vision for an organization (normally set by management) and general adherence and subscription to that vision or **culture** by employees. While, in reality, many organizations may attempt to develop and infuse **unitary** approaches, **Critical Management Studies** (CMS), in general, sees little value or authenticity in them. With regard to pluralism and **power** in **organizations**, pluralism generally sees this as taking the form of competing for and attempting to resolve conflicts of interest. It is possible that acts of **resistance** may result as a consequence of differences of opinion. Critical approaches tend to espouse and encourage pluralistic appreciations of organizational **cultures**.

Key Words:

Unitary, Voice.

References

Jones (2003); Learmouth (2008).

Politics

In the broadest sense, politics concerns the process of governing, and holding **authority** over a situation. Politics is seen as part of **discourse** and discursive process. Early work by Gouldner (1954) and Crozier (1964) has led on to a wide range of contemporary commentaries in relation to management, organization and politics (see some examples in Clegg, Courpasson and Phillips, 2006; Badham and Buchanan, 2009). Politics is inextricably associated with **agency** and the exercise, structuring and transformation of **power** (see **structure**). This goes hand in hand with the recognition that where different points of view and subjectivities are at play (and this is nearly always the case when numbers of individuals gather together) political activity and behaviour is almost unavoidable (see **subjectivity**).

Key Words:

Authority, Discourse, Power, Subjectivity.

References

Buchanan and Badham (2009); Clegg, Courpasson and Phillips (2006); Crozier (1964); Gouldner (1954); Mills, Mills and Thomas (2004).

Positivism

The origins of **positivism** are strongly associated with the French writer Auguste Comte (1798–1857). Comte was dissatisfied with the conventional and traditional epistemological assumptions (see **epistemology**) underlying existing ways used to understand major social phenomena such as, for example, poverty, social class and population growth. He wanted to generate an approach that would introduce scientific techniques and principles to the study of social dimensions and, consequently, he is often cited as one of the founders of the modern discipline of sociology. Comte's work has been built on and developed by many subsequent commentators and philosophers. Nevertheless, certain epistemological values have come to be seen as underpinning positivistic approaches (Bryman and Bell, 2007). These include: the use of empirical observation to record data; independence – a valuing of freedom for research from political constraints or interference, the creation of **hypotheses** and the deduction of data in relation to these **hypotheses**; an espousal of **determinism** (i.e. a belief in cause and effect); the opportunity to attempt some **reductionism** and generalization; and, the possibility of cross-analysis between different groups and entities (see **empiricism**, **political** and **deductivism**).

If, for example, a researcher is electing to adopt a positivistic approach in his or her research, he or she is likely to do all that is possible to follow a logical experiment-like process and employ **deductive** reasoning. At the same time, he or she will be seeking to maintain the **objectivity** of the research by trying to stop what might be viewed by others as

subjective opinions and assumptions from impacting on the study. Positivism is just one methodological **paradigm** of many. As indicated above, it has its own epistemological characteristics – that is ways of constructing and validating knowledge (see **epistemology**). Unlike in CMS, positivism has been widely adopted and employed in **normative** and **mainstream** research. Alternative methodological approaches, each having its own epistemological commitments, have tended to be used in critical approach research and writing.

Key Words:

Deductivism, Experimentation, Hypothesis, Objectivity, Reductionism.

References

Bryman and Bell (2007); Clegg, Kornberger and Pitsis (2008).

Postcolonialism

The initial wave of, what is generally referred to as, colonialism took place primarily in the late eighteenth century until the mid-twentieth century. Colonialism and colonization are processes of occupation, annexation and domination of other countries and cultures by, typically, Western powers. Postcolonialism is concerned with the subsequent consequences and impacts of colonialism and colonization.

The study of postcolonialism has grown out of the broader areas of humanities and social sciences. In particular, Said (1978) has been a central figure in the development of this field and has illustrated how, for example, the East (or more simultaneously 'exotically' and provocatively termed 'The Orient') is a construct of Western commentary and **gaze** (see **social constructionism**). One consequence of this is the **appropriation** of indigenous **voices** and **identities**, and processes of 'othering' (see **other**) by a host of officials, observers and Western writers. This leads to the production and **reproduction** of a romanticized and essentially false image of the colonialized country. However, equally, it may also be the case that many inhabitants of the colonized country align with, participate in and collaborate with these processes of **social constructionism** and **sense-making**.

Postcolonial theory has a presence in **Critical Management Studies** (CMS), although it is not perhaps as expansive as the quantity of work being undertaken in wider social science fields and departments. For illustrations of CMS-related accounts providing various insights into postcolonialism see Banerjee and Linstead (2004), Jack and Westwood (2009), Stokes and Gabriel (2010).

Key Words:

Appropriation, Gaze, Identity, Other, Reproduction, Social Constructionism, Voice.

References

Banerjee and Linstead (2004); Jack and Westwood (2009); Said (1978); Stokes and Gabriel (2010).

Post-Fordism (see this term in relation to Fordism)

Postmodernism

Postmodernism is a very complex and multifaceted phenomenon. As an initial or potential point of departure it can be said to be a philosophical approach that offers relativistic and subjectivity-informed critiques that contest and challenge rigid and fixed views of the world offered by philosophies such as **modernism** and rationalism (see **rationality**). However, to suggest that postmodernism is born uniquely out of a reaction to **modernism** would be oversimplistic. Postmodernism has generated multiple avenues of enquiry and commentary. It has evolved, transformed and even, in some ways, is incorporated into, or appropriated by, **modernism** and modernistic practices in organizations (Dereli and Stokes, 2007) (see **appropriation**). Postmodernism generally adheres to an emergent, subjective and non-linear **ontology**, **epistemology** and way of making sense of situations and contexts (see **emergence**, **subjectivity**, **linearity** and **sense-making**). It readily challenges boundaries, 'grand **narratives**' or **meta-narratives** approaches (see Lyotard, 1979) to developing understanding (see **boundary**). Postmodernism characterizes these traits as representationalist, fixed, unchanging and typically tending to be aligned with a more modernistic approach to understanding organizations (see **representation**).

It is very difficult to chart the **emergence** and development of postmodernism in relation to a particular era or epoch. Nevertheless, it is important to note a number of French philosophers' writing during the twentieth century including, for example, Jean Baudrillard (1929–2007) and Jean-François Lyotard (1924–1998). Postmodernism, as with **modernism**, can still be sensed in the contemporary world as a force employed in attempts to understand and construct the world in which we live. For instance, a number of authors, including Baudrillard (1988) and Best and Kellner (1991), have argued how media coverage of warfare in the contemporary era has become little more than presentations, or set of media images and diagrams, that substitute for **lived experience** and in so doing become a new alternative **reality** or simulation (or as Baudrillard termed it *simulacra*).

This ontological relativism (see **ontology**) of postmodernism continues to raise concerns and questions about how it can help **organizations** and **managers**. One of the reasons for this is that it is difficult to imagine **managers** and employees having to acknowledge that few things are 'real', fixed or unchanging. Indeed, it might be argued that the human condition needs a sense that some things are stable, at least for a period of time (however temporary or illusory) in order to be able to progress with some sense of purpose, direction and security. This may go some way partially to explain why postmodernism has had limited success penetrating or modifying **mainstream** or **normative** approaches. Equally, while postmodernism, might, by its adherents, be perceived as a force to challenge a **hegemonic modernism**, it cannot be overlooked that postmodernism itself is devoid of **power** and **hegemonic** effects and consequences in the way it seeks to assert the credentials of its philosophy. Although postmodernism has always had its opponents, nowadays, in organization and management studies, postmodernism is rarely offered as a utopian or ideal antidote to other ways of being or seeing the world as might have been the case 10 or 15 years ago (see Thompson, 1993) (see **utopia**).

Key Words:

Appropriation, Boundaries, Emergence, Linearity, Modernism, Rationality, Subjectivity, Utopia.

References

Allard-Poesi (2005); Baudrillard (1988); Best and Kellner (1991); Dereli and Stokes, (2007); Fleetwood (2005); Lyotard (1979); Thompson (1993).

Poststructuralism (also post-structuralism)

Poststructuralism initially emerged primarily in France in the 1960s and is associated with a number of writers and philosophers including Deleuze (1925–1995), Kristeva (1941–), Foucault (1926–1984) and Derrida (1930–2004). The key recurrent concerns and themes of poststructuralism embrace the ways in which **language** creates **reality** and in particular how **language**, **emotion** and sensory perceptions make human beings feel and behave in particular ways regarding the words they are hearing or seeing. Furthermore, we need to be mindful of how some forms of **language** may push aside other **language** possibilities that may be used to express and discuss a situation.

Poststructuralism is a relativist and non-essentialist way of under-standing the world and human relations. It is centrally concerned with the relationship to how **discourses** interact and interplay with concepts and the operation of **power**. For example, Foucault (as did other com-mentators, for example Bourdieu) portrayed **power** as fluid and organic rather than fixed or in a particular relationship of one person continu-ously holding power over, or in relation to, another. In other words, **power** is not just a top-down hierarchical effect (see **hierarchy**). It is continuously present and shifting in many different ways and places throughout a given organization and the people in it. This underlines a further feature of poststructuralist approaches – the de-centring of the subject (be it person or **institution**). In a world or environment seen as primarily discursive (see **discourse**), subjects become entities through which effects such as **power** move in a transitory manner. We should not, for example, see ourselves as *holding* **power** – rather it passes through and around us.

In the 1980s and 1990s, the work of Michel Foucault was particularly present in **Critical Management Studies** (CMS) organization and man-agement texts (see *inter alia* useful reviews by: Jermier, Knights and Nord, 1994; Knights, 2002). Foucault undertook a historical consideration of a number of **institutions** – prisons, asylums and mental hospitals – which led him to find parallels with other **institutions** such as schools, army barracks and universities (Foucault, 1975/1979). This work has been built on in subsequent decades to such an extent that a range of points and principles of his work have played a role in many management and organizational behaviour programmes. The manner in which cer-tain schools of organization and management **theory** have employed Foucauldian thought has been strongly criticized in some quarters for being disingenuous or inauthentic (for example, see Wray-Bliss' (2002) critique of the way **Labour Process Theory** has engaged Foucault's ideas).

In summary, postructuralism has provided an important critical ana-lytical approach with which to critique **normative** and **mainstream** management. However, these critiques also raise concerns that there are limits to how far **language** can portray **reality**. If language-created reality becomes so idiosyncratic, then it is difficult to see how it might be possible to develop a generalized sense of firm, useable findings and recommendations that practitioners can use. Furthermore, a focus on **language** means that researchers need to make **truth** claims regarding what **language** might mean, whereas interpretively (see **interpretivism**), it might be more suitable to ask respondents what they aim to say. Therefore, poststructuralism, in a similar manner to **postmodernism**, has, by its very nature and ideological commitments, proved a difficult domain around which to develop and maintain clearly outlined and fixed positions (see **ideology**). This should not, perhaps, be surprising given the ephemeral and fluid nature of the concepts underpinning it. Compounding these complexities, key writers (such as Foucault) have variously disowned and moved away from positions they have previously espoused. They have done this allegedly in response to what the term has come to (mis-)**represent**.

Key Words:

Discourse, Language, Power, Postmodernism, Reality, Representation, Subjectivity.

References

Contu, Driver and Jones (2010, in press); Foucault (1975/1979); Jermier, Knights and Nord (1994), Jones (2009, 2010, in press); Knights (2002), Willmott (2005), Wray-Bliss (2002).

Power

In its most general sense, power can be described as the possibility, control and ability to do something. It can also point at having **authority** over something or somebody. Modernistic (see **modernism**) views of **organizations** tend to see legitimate **authority** and power as being rooted in the role of management. **Critical Management Studies** (CMS) perspectives would tend to see this perspective as managerialist potentially leading to **appropriation**, oppression or **silencing** of employee or individual's **voices** (see **managerialism**). Alternatively, modernistic and managerialistic style approaches to **organizations** can sometimes handover a degree of power and responsibility to employees, thus offering them what is termed **empowerment**.

Clearly, the topic and analysis of power has been an enduring one, not just in **organization** and management studies but as a feature of human history overall. In organization and management, early influences on the subject of power include Weber and Marx who examined the role or power and **authority** in emerging bureaucratic forms, capitalist systems and societies (see **Marxism**, **capitalism** and **bureaucracy**). Subsequent significant contributions were made by, for example, Lukes

(1974) on '**radical**' power and Foucault (1977) on 'disciplinary' power (see **discipline**) showing how power and the effects of power are not so much 'held' but rather transitory and reproductive (see reproduction). In contemporary critical perspective writings on **power** and organizations there is a wealth material available on this rich and complex topic (see *inter alia*: Clegg, Courpasson and Phillips, 2006; Fineman, 2007; Buchanan and Badham, 2009; Clegg and Haugaard, 2009).

Key Words:

Authority, Appropriation, Empowerment, Managerialism, Modernism, Silencing, Voices.

References

Buchanan and Badham (2009); Clegg, Courpasson and Phillips (2006); Clegg and Haugaard (2009); Fineman (2007); Foucault (1977); Lukes (1974); McCabe (2010).

Premodernism

As the term suggests, 'premodernism' concerns, to some extent, that which came before **modernism**. Premodernism broadly relates to the 'Ancients' period, for example, Ancient Greece, Ancient Rome and so on and so forth. Here, 'ancient' means the equivalent of antiquity or long ago and seeks to indicate that these periods were very different to what followed them. Ancient societies often made sense (see **sense-making**) of the world based on religions, **myths**, legends, superstition, inherited **authority** and hierarchical **power** bases (i.e. monarchs and privileged families) (see **hierarchy**).

Premodernism was followed by the subsequent designated periods of The Dark Ages and the Medieval Period which, in turn, saw the **emergence** of the epochs of The Renaissance, The Reformation and The **Enlightenment**. Emergent and following on from these, although the precise inception and development of them is cause for debate, were the phases described as **modernism** and **postmodernism**.

Many of the central characteristics of **modernism** (i.e. **rationality**, **linearity**, **objectivity**) were a reaction and attempt to counter the ideological commitments of much of premodernism (see **ideology**). For **Critical Management Studies** (CMS) and mainstream and normative approaches, albeit in different ways, the significance of premodernism is that it points at a different way of **sense-making** and creating **meaning** of the world. On occasion, this contrasts radically with epochs and philosophies that emerged subsequently. However, the legacy and contemporary influence of premodernistic values and ideas in architecture, medicine, mathematics and the sciences is undeniably substantial and enduring.

Key Words:

Ancient, Critical Management Studies, Enlightenment, Meaning, Modernism, Myths, Postmodernism, Poststructuralism, Reformation, Renaissance, Sense-making.

References

Cummings (2002); Kavanagh, Kuhling and Keohane (2008); Korczynski (2005).

Privilege

As a *noun*, in everyday **language**, 'privilege' means possessing some form of benefit or advantage. As a *verb* it means to confer or give an advantage to somebody or something. It is in this latter sense that the expression '… to privilege X…' is more often than not used in critical management writing. **Critical Management Studies** (CMS) is particularly interested in the ways in which certain situations, contexts, agents and **discourses** become privileged, or operate in a privileged manner in relation to other individuals, groups or situations (see **agency**). In *being privileged* they create, assume and employ **power**, and the effects of power, in order to control and even **silence** and oppress **others** (see Wray-Bliss, 2004).

Key Words:

Agency, Discourses, Oppression, Others, Power, Silence.

References

Boogaard and Roggeband (2010); Stokes and Gabriel (2010); Voronov (2008); Wray-Bliss (2004).

Qq Rr

Race

Race is a complex and extensive subject that has received increasing attention in the contemporary era. As an initial definitional point, a race of people is a group of people sharing common origins, beliefs and possibly, although this is a difficult area in relation to race, genetics. As a term, 'race' might, in certain contexts, also be viewed as something not fixed but ultimately determined by human choices, actions and decisions. In other words, it can be perceived as a social construction (see **social constructionism**) of similarities and differences between human beings. In some circumstances, the creation, **reproduction** and reinforcement of these felt characteristics can lead to discrimination or prejudice based on grounds of race. There are regrettably many examples of racism in ancient and contemporary history alike. Two such examples include the systematic racism perpetrated by the Nazi Third Reich in relation to Jews, ethnic minorities and vulnerable groups; and, more contemporaneously, the Apartheid regime that separated whites and blacks in South Africa for many years.

It can clearly be seen that race and racism relate to **identity** in an inextricable and direct manner. 'Who' individuals think they are and wish to be, in conjunction with how other people portray them, all play a role in the construction of **identity**. The **power** to cast others in a particular light, or 'othering' (see **other**), can be a dangerous and potent act leading to **alienation** and destruction. It is in this frame of reference that critical approaches have analysed and considered issues of race and diversity in relation to organization and management. On the other hand,

normative and **mainstream** perspectives tend to engage with issues of race and **diversity** in the sense that they are things that need to be managed in order to make the firm more effective, efficient and improve **performativity**. In particular, in relation to contemporary national legal regimes and work settings, there are a wide selection of laws focusing on equal opportunities, human rights and race relations. These have been introduced with the aim of developing fairness of treatment and avoidance of prejudice.

One area concerning issues of race that is worthy of mention, and which has emerged within the critical umbrella of wider social sciences, has been the field of **postcolonialism**. This analyses **power** relations and portrayal of various racial groups and indigenous populations in colonial contexts (Banerjee and Linstead, 2004; Jack and Westwood, 2009).

Key Words:

Alienation, Discrimination, Diversity, Equal Opportunities, Identity, Other, Prejudice, Reproduction, Social Constructionism.

References

Banerjee and Linstead (2004); Jack and Westwood (2009).

Radical

This term evokes the idea of revolutionary, total, rapid and thorough change and departure from what has gone before. In some regards, the notion of extreme may be associated with radical.

Critical Management Studies (CMS) is likely to be considered by a range of observers and commentators (particularly from **mainstream** and **normative** stances) as proposing relatively, and on occasion quite, radical insights and perspectives on organizational life. These differences can lead to tensions between the domains. Various attempts have been made by authors to chart diverse philosophical stances in relation to organization and management studies. One such oft-cited work is that of Burrell and Morgan (1979) (see the entry on **paradigm**). A key radical aim of CMS is the **emancipation** of individuals in the workplace – its research subjects. Often this takes the form of micro-**emancipations** which are localized and idiosyncratic rather than occurring on a more widespread scale (as in the case of, for example, a whole social class as commonly proposed in **Marxism** with regard to the working class or proletariat) (Spicer, Alvesson and Kärreman, 2009).

Key Words:

Critical Management Studies, Emancipation, Mainstream, Marxism, Normative.

References

Burrell and Morgan (1979); Carey (2009); Spicer, Alvesson and Kärreman (2009); Willmott (2005).

Rationality

Rationalism is a belief system that sees great value in the principles and employment of linear logic and **objectivity** in addressing issues and problems (see **linearity**). It rejects many of the ideas of premodernistic thinking (see **premodernism**). Rationalism forms a central part of the philosophies of **modernism** and **positivism** in **normative** and **mainstream** management and **organization** approaches. Such approaches are seen, by their adherents, as constituting the best way of achieving efficient, effective and performative organizations (see **performativity**). Employing rationality, **mainstream** approaches are often confident that some form of ideal, neutral and apolitical stance or solution in relation to data and factual discovery is being accomplished (see **politics**).

Key Words:

Apolitical, Control, Fact, Logic, Mainstream, Modernism, Normative, Objectivity, Stability.

References

Casey (2004); Higgins and Tamm-Hallström (2007); Thompson and McHugh (2009).

Reality

Reality concerns issues of existence and being. Questions of reality have been at the heart of human thinking and discussion for much of history. Debates and analysis on reality belong to the area of philosophy called **ontology**. Ontology is a field that is concerned with discussing the nature of reality that is what reality *is* or *might be*.

For a large number of people in everyday life their view of reality is a given and they are unlikely to question it. In this way of seeing the world, a house is obviously a house, a job is a job, a thought is a thought and a conversation is a conversation and so on and so forth, and 'facts', ideas, characteristics, categories, names and labels pertaining to these notions and people are already assigned, fixed and established. They are simply 'out there' waiting to be discovered as and when research (scientific) techniques and advances will allow. Ontologically, such a view falls within a positivistic and rationalist way of seeing the world. It sees itself as objective and free from bias or being influenced by individual values (see **positivism, rationalism, positivism, reductionism**). Rationalism and **positivism** do not accord a strong role for **subjectivity** or human emotion, personality or individual perspective (see **rationality**).

However, alternative perspectives such as, for example, **Social Constructionism, Postmodernism, Poststructuralism** and **Critical Realism** take differing ontological views on reality. These perspectives tend to see reality as being 'made' by human interaction and perception and the interplay of **subjectivity, language** and **discourses**. For approaches such as these, reality is not necessarily fixed and unchanging, rather it is created and prone to constantly being made and remade as contexts and **discourses** transform. Although it is difficult to generalize in such a rich and complex sphere, **Critical Management Studies** (CMS) tends to subscribe to a more subjective, emergent and constructionist way of making sense of reality (see **subjectivity, emergence, social construction** and **sense-making**).

Key Words:

> Ontology, Positivism, Postmodernism, Poststructuralism, Rationalism, Scientific Techniques, Sense-Making, Social Constructionism.

References

> Ackroyd and Fleetwood (2001); Fletcher and Watson (2007); Woźniak (2010).

Reductionism

Reductionism is the process whereby complex and sophisticated issues, objects, situations and environments are attempted to be broken down into the elements that constitute them. Reductionism has at its core the aim and belief that by breaking things down it will be easier to analyse and understand them. Reductionism is a central characteristic and process of logical, rationalistic and positivistic approaches (see **rationality** and **positivism**).

Critics of reductionism suggest that the attempt and process of simplifying complex problems means that there is a risk that some things may be distorted, marginalized or overlooked. Reductionism and the positivistic process of analysing data often involve drawing boundaries and categories in data, **experiences** and observations (see **boundary**). For those commentators who question the validity of reductionism, their queries and charges tend to centre on how, what, when and who is making the decisions on where such divisions are drawn.

Nevertheless, equally, it might be argued that in many instances some form of reductionism takes place in most analyses – even in critical approaches. It might be said that to be able to discuss something we need terms and labels to indicate and point at the topic or issues. In other words, we need to be able to represent it (see **representation**). However, in general, critical approaches tend to adopt a more cautious descriptive approach that considers a range of possibilities, insights and attempts to portray possible **meanings** and interpretations. This contrasts with the prescriptive closure (i.e. saying how things *should or ought to be*, or be done) of more reductionist stances. Alternatively expressed, objectifying and positivistic approaches to analysis often seem insensitive, or on occasion possibly even unaware, of the lines drawn in the systems of classification and categorization they invoke. However, such concerns are likely to remain foremost in the mind of the critical commentator.

Key Words:

Categories, Classifications, Boundaries, Description, Positivism, Prescription, Rationality, Representation.

References

Al-Amoudi (2007); Fairhurst (2004).

Reflexivity

Reflexivity is the process which recognizes and acknowledges implications of the relationships and interactions between the researcher and research respondents. Simultaneously, symbiotically and reciprocally, the researcher and the research respondents are likely to **experience** and be affected by the process of the research and this is turn affects the data and the findings. For example, in a research project the researcher may be involved in studying and questioning research respondents or participants using, for instance, **participant observation**. Many would argue that the respondents are inevitably and irreversibly affected by having met and known the researcher; that is, once he or she has entered the lives of the researched through the project, his or her impact and the memory of him or her plays a role in the respondents' lives – they co-create each other. Equally, the respondents or research participants are likely to have a similar impact on the researcher.

Reflexivity is one of the recurrent central principles of **Critical Management Studies** (CMS) approaches (Fournier and Grey, 2000; Alvesson and Sköldberg, 2009). It is seen as playing an important role in the inductive and interpretive-style research that CMS frequently employs (see **inductivism** and **interpretivism**). However, reflexivity and the attendant issues of **power** and control have also raised a number of concerns about CMS researchers, including the point that they are prone to appropriating the **voices** of research respondents rather than emancipating or enabling them (see Wray-Bliss and Brewis, 2008) (see **appropriation** and **emancipation**). Due to the subjective dimensions and aspects of reflexivity it tends not to play a role in the deductive and positivistic methodological processes that broadly underpin **mainstream** and **normative** approaches (see **subjectivity**, **deductivism** and **positivism**).

Key Words:

Appropriation, Inductivism, Interpretivism, Subjectivity, Voice.

References

Alvesson and Sköldberg (2009); Fournier and Grey (2000); Rhodes and Brown (2005); Waddington (2004); Wray-Bliss and Brewis (2008).

Reification

'Reification' is a term periodically employed in **Critical Management Studies** (CMS) texts and means the process whereby objects, concepts or events are discussed as if they had came into existence without human involvement. In other words, they are talked about as if they were completely independent, solid and 'real' (see **reality**) outside of human experience in relation to them. Examples of such phenomena might be the idea of technological innovation, corporate **culture** or bureaucratic systems and **structures** (see **bureaucracy** and **determinism**). Of course, in one sense, all of these processes and aspects can be said to reside and 'exist' outside of, and independent to, human senses (see **ontology**). However, it can be argued that it is still human beings who label, represent, make sense of and give **meaning** to them (see **representation, sense-making**).

A couple of illustrations will assist in elaborating reification. For example, we may talk about an **organization** having a corporate **culture**, and indeed many meetings and actions may be taken in relation to it, but this does not mean that the essentially abstract concept of 'culture' *actually exists* as a coherent, stable, 'touchable' entity. Nevertheless, people in organizations frequently work on this assumption and thereby *reify* the concept that is operate as though it *exists* and *is* real. Equally, a further illustration of reification is in connection with talk of technology causing **radical** change in organizations that is technology shapes and determines change. Critical perspectives label this machine-driven perspective towards technology as *technological determinism* and because of the reification it involves it is seen as flawed or partial. Critical approach adherents point out that the perspectives, constructions, perceptions, behaviours, decisions and **sense-making** people create around the technological objects and systems are just as likely to produce change effects and impressions as the hardware itself. Overall, critical approaches are very cautious and critical of acts of reification frequently identified in **mainstream** and **normative** texts.

Key Words:

Mainstream, Meaning, Normative, Ontology, Sense-Making, Structure, Reality, Representation.

References

Hellström (2004); Ogber (2000).

Representation

Representationalism, or the act of representing something, can be viewed as a process of talking about and labelling an artefact or concept as if it has a consequent solidity, concreteness and existence independent of human perception, action or experience. **Normative** and **mainstream** approaches commonly and regularly engage in acts of representation and representationalism. These are seen as usual ways of approaching the development of **knowledge** for these perspectives (see also for further elaboration; **deductivism, epistemology, modernism, ontology, positivism, rationalism, reification**).

Critical approaches commonly see representation as potentially problematic. Critical perspectives recognize that labels and referents (i.e. objects that are the subject of terms and names) are important (if not to some degree an unavoidable precursor) to being able to have a discussion about them. However, they are simultaneously very wary of what such labelling acts include and exclude. Critical perspectives are also concerned about impacts such as the creation of boundaries and *othering* (see **boundary** and **others**). Equally, they are very engaged in considering issues of **power** and **appropriation** of **voice** that acts of representation and representationalism can produce and reproduce (see **reproduction**).

Key Words:

Epistemology, Mainstream, Modernism, Normative, Ontology, Positivism, Rationalism, Reification.

References

Ellis (2008); Matanle, McCann and Ashmore (2008); Mescher, Benschop and Dooreward (2010); Phillips and Rippin (2010).

Reproduction

When something that has already been made (i.e. produced) or has taken place is made again or the act repeated it is said to be *reproduced*. In critical approaches the idea of reproduction is commonly used to show how a situation, or the given effects and consequences of a situation, are made to happen again because the person(s), **organization** or **institution** to whom they originally happened goes on to (re-)produce the actions and effects in a fresh situation. This observation is usually made in relation to discussions on **power** and the ways in which power functions. The idea of the effects of power and **discipline** in organizational and institutional settings being reproduced is an important theme in the work of the French philosopher Michel Foucault (1926–1984) (see also **postmodernism, poststructuralism**) and has been employed in a wide range of critical analyses. A further illustration, although not the only one possible, of reproduction in action might be the instance where aggressive or bullying behaviours are present in an organization. This has the effect of 'informing' or 'educating' other individuals that these behaviours are normal or **normative** in that given context and some individuals, influenced by this, reproduce these behaviours in their own conduct towards others.

Key Words:

Discipline, Postmodernism, Poststructuralism, Power.

References

Finn (2008); Kerr and Robinson (2009); Riach (2007).

Resistance

When we think of resistance we generally think of *reacting against* control imposed by something or someone on a person, organization or context. Resistance usually implies dissent by one person or group towards another which may, in turn, lead to conflict. Resistance can take a range of forms or patterns. One way (but certainly not the only way) of thinking about resistance is in a **spatial** manner that is *where* it takes place. For example, is resistance occurring from within or *inside* (i.e. by employees or trades unions) or from outside the **organization** (i.e. shareholders, protesters, lobbyists)? Alternatively, in **temporal** terms, it can involve a one-off act, or a series of events, by an individual or group. Resistance may be comprised of a physical act, such as protesting or standing up to make a speech or point. Alternatively, it might take a more passive approach consisting of, for example, the act of simply not getting involved or withdrawing participation, from an initiative or meeting.

Trades unions might be seen as a formalized structure that can offer resistance. And, it is indeed a fact that, for a range of reasons, trade union activism and membership numbers have reduced in recent years compared to preceding decades. Nevertheless, it is also important to recognize that resistance continues as an integral and implicit part of many workplace relationships. Collinson (1994) argued that while workers may not have *formal* **authority** (for example, **power** invested in managerial roles) nevertheless they do possess **power** in relation to **knowledge** of such things as technical approaches and processes. Workers at all levels have the possibility of exerting resistance and **power** through the basis of this **knowledge**. Collinson points at two typical forms this resistance might take. Firstly, there is *resistance by distance*. This will involve, for example, the denial of, or not passing on, information that workers posses to managerial or directive tiers thereby rendering management decision-making and operation less efficient. In a further strategy, workers might employ *resistance through persistence*. Here, for example, workers may aim to engage and solicit information constantly from management which may serve to keep management on the 'back foot'. Reciprocally, however, management may choose to engage selectively with information dissemination and contact as they think appropriate.

We may also see *game-playing* as part of an approach to resistance. Ackroyd and Thompson in their (1999) work *Organizational Misbehaviour* show that for some employees game-playing and resistance against managerial control is a way of relieving boredom and monotony at work – a kind of sport. **Organizations** often stipulate aims, visions and missions and advocate particular values and beliefs in a **unitary** manner on behalf of the corporate enterprise. The people who come to work in an organization are of course individuals in their own right and there is no guarantee that all the corporate values will marry with their own. Some people may openly **voice** their dissent or disagreement and this may lead to conflict with **managers**. Alternatively, some people may go through the motions of paying lip service to certain aspects of the firm rather than sincerely engaging with them. This is an example of one of the many games that people may decide to play as a subtle form of resistance in the workplace.

Normative or **mainstream** approaches to management tend to view resistance as a negative act – a disturbance or disruption that needs to be overcome. On the other hand, critical perspectives view resistance from a range of alternative possibilities. **Critical Management Studies** (CMS) analyses of resistance invoke a range of complexities surrounding **identity**, **power**, sexuality, **structure** and **agency** to name but a few possible dimensions. Critical approaches are particularly interested and engaged in identifying resistance in local situations and data. Thus there are a wide range of studies that examine small, micro-situations such as a single office, factory or **organization** and portray various modes and forms of resistance that may be taking place therein and around it. It is perhaps a criticism of some CMS studies that, in discussing resistance, they have a tendency to homogenize 'the other side' or their target (such as '**managers**') rather than seeing them also as individuals as much as any other employee. Increasingly critical commentaries have striven to demonstrate that, rather than being some form of automaton, men and women who are in managerial roles are equally exercised and pressured by the attendant issues of resistance, **identity** and **power** (Fleming, 2007; Fleming and Spicer, 2007; Mills, Mills and Thomas, 2004).

Key Words:

Conflict, Dissent, Game-Playing, Organizational Behaviour, Power, Voice.

References

Ackroyd and Thompson (1999); Collinson (1994); Fleming (2007); Fleming and Spicer (2007); Jermier, Knights and Nord (1994); Kärreman and Alvesson (2009); Mills, Mills and Thomas (2004); Munro (2004); McCabe (2010).

Rhetoric

The history and tradition of rhetoric is a long-standing one going back to **premodern** ancient civilizations. Rhetoric is the art of effective communication and public speaking. In contemporary **language** it has, however, come to be understood, as flowery, exaggerated **language** which aims to impress. Calling a speech or text rhetorical may also mean that the words being spoken or written are insincere, shallow and empty of **meaning**. Rhetorical language and expression does little to advance genuine understanding and develop meaning.

All texts and pronouncements are in danger of employing rhetorical or clichéd language. Critical perspective critiques of **mainstream** texts frequently argue that the portrayals of managerial and organizational situations do not show a **reality** or **lived experience** that individuals in those settings would acknowledge or recognize (also see **boundary, reification, representation**). Typical illustrations might include, for example, accounts of '**organizations** as **unitary**', references to 'the faster and faster rate of change in **organizations** and the world', 'the need for **managers** to be reflective and empowering' and many more possible statements in a similar vein. Such statements are of course worthy of consideration; however, they are often represented in a way that is trite and fleeting (see **representation**).

It would be short-sighted to believe that critical accounts are devoid of rhetoric. The extensive use in critical accounts of obtuse and dense sociological **language** to express ideas might be considered a form of rhetoric. Here, it might be argued that **language** is sometimes used to impress, or to indicate adherence to a particular lexicon and jargon of an elite.

Key Words:

Boundaries, *Cliché*, Language, Meaning, Premodern, Reification, Representation.

References

Dent (2003); Kitay and Wright (2007); Sillince and Brown (2009).

Rhizome (adjective: rhizomatic)

'Rhizome' is a term derived from the natural sciences that refers to plant stems that sprout spasmodically from a plant root and spread horizontally and extensively through the ground. Thus, nodes spontaneously project out from various points of the plant and spread, interweave and interconnect. In **organization** and management, rhizome is used in a **metaphorical** sense to point at forms of organizing and **organization** that behave, form and reform in a similar manner to rhizomatic plant roots and nodes. This **representation** contrasts to more traditional and hegemonic hierarchical ways of considering organization which tend to function in a more vertical and linear fashion and **structure** (see **hegemony**, **hierarchy**, **linearity**). Blaug (1999) provides a range of examples to illustrate rhizomatic organizational phenomena including the manner in which many communist states in Eastern Europe at the end of the 1980s and early 1990s were overturned; the spontaneous rising up of the population in the French Revolution and the development of guerrilla wars against imperial and state forces.

In contemporary organizational settings, rhizomatic patterns can be seen in informal communication, **structures** and actions incorporating gossip and grapevine communication and tacit collaborations and **resistance** in relation to more overt, formal **structures** and **authority** of the **organizations**. In another sense, aspects of the **emergence** and development of the Internet may also be viewed as rhizomatic. Key commentators in this area were Gilles Deleuze (1925–1995) and Felix Guattari (1930–1992). In their writings, **organizations** were analysed as neural networks rather than tree-like root, trunk, branch, leaf fixed **structures**. Within rhizomatic forms of organizing, neural patterns, micro-operations and small group actions (rather than the oft-vaunted grand strategic plans) become very important for determining outcomes. Among their most influential texts was *A Thousand Plateaus: Capitalism and Schizophrenia* (1987).

Due to their unpredictable nature, rhizomatic **structures** are difficult to subject to control. If there were an attempt to adopt a rhizomatic approach as the dominant (hegemonic) way of organizing, it would not necessarily respond well to, or provide, manager requirements for predictable information and outcomes (see **hegemony**). However, a range of commentators and observers suggest that organizational action and development may well be more rhizomatic in nature than traditional views of structure portray and suggest (Santana and Carpentier, 2009).

Key Words:

Hegemonic, Metaphor, Modal.

References

Blaug (1999); Clegg, Kornberger and Rhodes (2005); Deleuze and Guattari (1987); Linstead and Pullen (2006); Santana and Carpentier (2009).

Ritual

A ritual is a set pattern or order of events and actions that takes place over a given period of time. Rituals are a central part of human **experience**. Rituals often have formalities and standardized procedures but they can also be unofficial and informal (Turner, 1969). For example, a formal procedure might be the monthly sales meeting in a company, or periodic celebrations of 'employee of the month'. More, informally, there may well be patterns and habits that some employees engage in such as going off for breakfast, breaks at a certain time or regularly meeting up at a bar or pub after work. In different national **cultures** various rituals can be identified. For instance, in a French office it is expected that on arrival at the organization a colleague will shake hands with all those present before commencing work. In a Japanese factory, morning group exercises may be run for everyone to join in.

Rituals are much more than comprising a simple act. Rituals contain and convey **symbolism**, **meaning** and significance for those involved in them and also those who witness them. Participating in rituals shows that you are part of a given group and that you are *socialized* into that community. Rituals have played a role in a range of organizational models particularly in relation to discussions on corporate **culture** – see for example Johnson's (1992) model of the 'Cultural Web' and also Deal and Kennedy (1982) and Carter and Muller (2002).

Key Words:

Meaning, Socialization, Symbolism.

References

Carter and Muller (2002); Deal and Kennedy (1982); Johnson (1992); Lawrence (2004); Turner (1969).

Ss

Scientific Management

Scientific Management is an approach to analysing and designing work processes that was pioneered by Frederick W. Taylor (1856–1915). Taylor was profoundly concerned at the wastage and inefficiency he witnessed in factory working practices. The **ideology** and set of principles he developed for organizing workplaces and processes would become known as *Taylorism*. These principles include, for example: division of the work into constituent tasks, minimal handling of components and tools and the organization of labour into specialist tasks to tally with the work organization. Taylorism was embraced by the early Ford Motor Company and introduced into the company's production plants. Taylorism merged with mass production machines and techniques gave rise to **Fordism**.

From its inception Scientific Management was the cause of considerable conflict and disagreement often between employees on the one side and, on the other, management and owners. Workers felt that the techniques gave rise to deskilling, a challenge and breaking down of traditional craft approaches and task **organization.** On occasion this ultimately gave rise to worker **alienation** and **resistance**.

Although Scientific Management and Taylorism originated approximately 100 years ago, echoes of its principles and practices can still be evidenced in many of today's work situations and sectors. Moreover, because of its scientific underpinning, Taylorism shares ideas of **rationality**, **positivism** and **modernism** with many aspects of contemporary **mainstream** management and **organization theory** and practice. As a contemporary illustration of Taylorism, customer call centres are often considered to provide a clear example. Equally, the application of Taylorism is at the heart of the modern phenomenon labelled **McDonaldization.** This embraces a wide range of activity including not only fast food but also provision for health and education.

Key Words:

Alienation, Control, Division of Labour, Fordism, Ideology, Mainstream, McDonald-ization, Modernism, Rationality, Resistance.

References

Frenkel (2005); Linstead, Fulop and Lilley (2009).

Semiotics (adjective: semiotics)

'Semiotic(s)' is the term given to the study of signs and symbols especially in relation to the role they play in **language** (see **symbolism**). Semiotics is of recurrent interest to critical approaches because, given the wide span of sociological, philosophical, reflexive, discursive approaches and concepts they engage, there is extensive scope for rich analyses and interpretation (see **reflexivity** and **discourse**). **Mainstream** accounts, on the other hand, tend to look at symbols and signs in a more literal, deterministic and reductionist manner (see **determinism** and **reductionism**).

Key Words:

Language, Mainstream, Signs, Symbols (Symbolism).

References

Elmes and Frame (2008); Hancock (2005); Rosenthal and Peccei (2006).

Sense-making

The ways and manners in which people develop an understanding of the world through their personal histories, contexts and **experiences** constitute how they create **meaning**. In this vein, the concept of sense-making has received increasing attention in the social sciences during the last 30 years. In relation to organization and management, the work of, among others, Karl Weick (1995) has been an important influence.

Sense-making involves how individuals look at the current and contemporary events that are taking place around them in order to see how they relate to previous **experience**. In doing this, it is quite commonplace for people to relate their experiences to **stories** linking them with other **narratives** they know or things they have experienced. This, in turn, has consequences for constructing people's identities and **Weltanschauung** (world view(s)) (see **social constructionism** and **identity**).

Weick suggests that there are a number of characteristics involved in processes of sense-making, namely:

- *Ongoing* – we never stop making sense;
- *Retrospective* – we look backwards over the past to be able to understand;
- *Plausible* – sense-making is never perfect, it is makeshift and ongoing just for the purposes of temporary understanding;
- makes full use of *images* when we sense-make – we make sketches, draw pictures with our hands, and generally try to **represent** things;
- *Rationalize* – we use logic and we simplify to be able to comprehend (see **rationality**);
- *People*, not things, undertake sense-making;
- *Doing* and talking help us to provide the 'raw materials' to work through what we are trying to understand.

Key Words:

Experience, Identities, Meaning, Narratives, Represent, Social Constructionism, Stories, Weltanschauung.

References

Allard-Poesi (2005); Brown, Stacey and Nandhakumar (2008); Taylor and Robichaud (2004); Weick (1995).

Silence (also silencing)

Silence concerns the absence of sound or noise. It can also mean that something is not being said because it is being avoided because it is being impeded or blocked from being uttered or shown. The state or condition of silence is therefore clearly connected to the idea of **voice** and the possibility, or not, for a **voice** to be expressed or heard.

In the workplace it might often be the case that given individuals or groups feel that they are being silenced – unable to express their ideas and views. This can happen in a range of ways, for example, by being omitted from emails or communications, by not being invited to meetings or not included in correspondence. Silencing may not necessarily be deliberate. It may be inadvertent on the part of the person who is causing the silencing to take place. It might equally be produced by insensitivity or incompetence. The presence of silence in a workplace may suggest that some form of bullying, harassment or oppressive behaviour is taking place. In pluralistic (see **pluralism**) work environments (as opposed to **unitary**) it is perhaps more likely to witness a range of voices in operation in debates and discussions. While pluralistic environments may appear more libertarian, this does not mean that silencing cannot and does not sometimes occur within them.

Key Words:

Oppression, Pluralism, Unitary, Voice.

References

Bowen and Blackmon (2003); Park and Keil (2009); Simpson and Lewis (2005).

Social constructionism

Social constructionism is a philosophical approach to understanding how people make sense of, and act in relation to, other people, their interactions and the contexts in which these take place. It holds that people interact with each other to create **meaning** of the world (see **sense-making**). Of course, interaction take places through numerous forms of **discourse** and exchange including through the senses of sight, sound, touch, smell and hearing and also by means of, for example, **symbols**, sights, music, texts, posters, **body language**, words and conversations. This coalesces into an individual *Weltanschauung* (a term taken from German meaning 'world view') which sees **sense-making** as emergent as context, perceptions and understandings are constantly formed and reformed as people make and remake their understanding of the world. For instance, concepts such as 'culture' are 'produced' as a consequence of such interaction and, in turn, the norms and habitual patterns (and irregularities in relation to that) reproduce behaviours and **meanings** (see **reproduction**).

Berger and Luckmann (1966) produced the influential text *The Social Construction of Reality* which sought to provide an account of how reality might be constructed. For Berger and Luckmann the process of the *objectification* of knowledge building is a consequence of intertwined processes of *typification* (classifying and 'agreeing' knowledge) and subsequent *habitualization* (repeated usage and reinforcement) which give rise to the '*externalization*' and '*objectification*' (the rendering as 'fact' of something) of human and social **experience**. In turn, this permits a process of consequent *internalization* of a created '**reality**' in that: 'A world so regarded attains a firmness in consciousness'(ibid.: p. 78). And, as such, everyday human experiences become seen as 'legitimated' (ibid.: p. 111) or '**representations**' rather than being 'humanly produced' (Berger and Luckmann, 1971: 78; Chia, 1996). It should not be assumed that 'these moments' occur in a progressive linear (see **linearity**) or strict '**temporal** sequence' (ibid.: p. 149) but rather through an iterative and relational manner (see also Watson and Harris 1999: 18 and Chia, 1996: 581). **Power** clearly has the potential to play an important role in a holistic comprehension of social construction. Interestingly, the lack of consideration of power in Berger and Luckmann's work is a common critique of their ideas.

In much **Critical Management Studies** (CMS) **discourse**, the **positivism** espoused by **mainstream** approaches and the associated **objectivity** are often seen as diametrically opposite to CMS' **subjective**, **relativist**, **interpretivist** and indeed social constructionist ways of seeing the world. At the more extreme end of this subjectivist spectrum, it is possible that a number of commentators would suggest that there is no such thing as 'solid' **reality** at all and even the physical sensations we receive when we make contact with an object, for example, shaking somebody's hand or bumping into something are themselves social constructions that are created within our minds rather than being physically real (see **reality**). Such intense relativistic positions form part of a position termed *solipsism*. Solipsism means that nothing at all offers a concrete or physical **reality** and everything is in emergent and in transition, even illusory (see **emergence**).

In many critical accounts, little is provided in the centrist ground between the two broad positions of an **objective positivism** and a **subjective interpretivism**. Nevertheless, **Critical Realism** has for a range of CMS commentators provided something of a 'middle terrain' wherein its adherents accept that **structures** and objects *exist*. In other words, in an ontological sense (see **ontology**) they have a solid **reality** separate from the observer and are not figments of the observer's imagination. However, simultaneously within **Critical**

Realism, individuals and groups of individuals interacting between each other, and in relation to **structures** and objects, create **meaning** and significance around those artefacts and **experiences**. In this way the object or experiences are 'constructed'. Watson (2008) has pointed at the need to be careful of the way in which social constructionism in relation to the fields of **poststructuralism** and **postmodernism** has been annexed primarily as a linguistic exercise detached from 'reality' by linguistic turns.

Key Words:

Externalization, Habitualization, Internalization, Interpretivism, Meaning, Reality, Sense-making, Typification.

References

Berger and Luckmann (1966); Chia (1996); Grint (2005); Rosenthal and Peccei (2006); Strati (1998); Watson (2008); Watson and Harris (1999).

Socialization

Socialization concerns how people become part of a section of a community, group of people or society. It is a concept examined extensively in the wider social sciences. For some commentators, socialization is said to consist of *primary* socializations (the **experiences** we have as a child with our parents or guardians) and *secondary* socializations (the subsequent **experiences** we have in nursery, schools, with groups of friends, work, college and university and so on and so forth). This dualistic representation is seen as too simplistic by some observers (see **dualism** and **representation**). Rather, socialization can be viewed as a complex concept involving the labyrinthine interaction of many aspects and **experiences** including **rituals**, routines, **discourses**, **language**, **semiotics** and **symbolism**. Each individual contributes to the development or construction (see **social constructionism**) of an overall atmosphere and context of a particular **culture** and, in turn, has **experiences** within, and in relation to, the group that inform and shape his or her **identity**. In these patterns, individuals are said to gradually *internalize* socio-cultural **experiences** and socio-cultural environments. Moreover, it is difficult to determine with any particular precision the role of particular agents, for example, parents, friends, teachers, work colleagues, managers and so on in bringing about socialization **experiences** (see **agency** and **actor network theory**) pointing up the highly subjective (see **subjectivity**) nature of the processes and experiences.

Socialization is not an unproblematized idea and a host of commentators find difficulties in talking about it as some form of process with solidity or clear boundaries (such as the categorizations of primary and secondary mentioned above) (see **boundary**). Nonaka and Takeuchi (1995) have highlighted the roles of tacit and explicit **knowledge** in relation to socialization processes underlining that it involves iterative transitions from tacit knowledge to explicit knowledge (rather than a more formal process) as **knowledge** is passed between people through behaviour and unwritten codes.

Key Words:

Actor Network Theory, Agency, Culture, Discourse, Identity, Knowledge, Language, Rituals, Semiotics, Subjectivity, Symbolism.

References

Friedland (2009); Hanlon (2004); Haski-Leventhal and Bargal (2008); Kuhn (2009); Nonaka and Takeuchi (1995).

Spatial

The adjective of space is spatial. Therefore, to use the expression, for example 'we need to consider the spatial aspects of X' means that to look at those parts of X that are concerned with, or relate to space, place or (physical) position. The term 'spatial' is not a term on which it is common to find a particular entry in a book, or in an index or contents list. It is a word used in the **language** and **discourse** of texts in **Critical Management Studies**-style (CMS) writing and tends not to be a term employed in more **normative** or **mainstream** commentaries. It is difficult to isolate the reason for this. Perhaps one possibility is that a term such as 'spatial' points up an attempt to talk about space in a more abstract, subjective and non-realist way as opposed to the objective, literal manner that is more usual in **mainstream** approaches (see **reality**, **subjectivity**, **objectivity** and **ontology**). Discussions on spatial aspects of topics, or objects, often go hand in hand with consideration of **temporal** (time-related) aspects. By considering the spatial- and temporal-related aspects in tandem it is possible to chart and discuss the character of something in the two key dimensions of space and time.

Key Words:

Critical Management Studies, Discourse, Language, Mainstream, Normative, Objectivity, Ontology, Subjectivity.

References

Borch (2010); Cremin (2010); Fleming and Spicer (2004).

Story (also storytelling)

A story is the telling or relating of a series of events in a sequence. Stories are also sometimes referred to as **narratives**, although there is argument surrounding various differences and definitions of the terms.

Stories are a long-standing and enduring dimension of human society and **experience**. They have become increasingly used in **organization** and management studies. Stories often help people to express **emotion**, make sense of **experiences** and develop **meaning** in relation to them (Fineman, 2003) (see **sense-making**). Moreover, stories employ the use of rich and complex **language**, **discourse**, **semiotics** and **symbolism** and centre on characters who have personalities and histories. While stories may be passed off as factual they are highly prone to embellishment and elaboration and involve highly imaginary and even aspects of fantasy. Equally, stories can enter the realm of **myth** wherein particular tales becomes 'legendary' in an **organization**.

A wide range of both **mainstream** (i.e. non-critical) and critical approaches to management and **organization** have employed story and storytelling approaches in recent decades (see, for example, Polkinghorne, 1988; Gabriel, 2000; Czarniawska, 1998, 2004; Boje, 2008). Stories have also been employed in the consultancy arena in health care sectors, government and emergency services as a way of understanding situations and contexts from different perspectives (see Dave Snowden's work on www.cognitive.edge.com (2010)).

Key Words:

Discourse, Experience, Language, Meaning, Narrative, Semiotics, Sense-making, Symbolism.

References

Boje (2008); Brown, Gabriel and Gherardi (2009); Czarniawska (1998, 2004); Fineman (2003); Gabriel (2000); Polkinghorne (1988); Watson (2009).

Structure

A structure is a construction, building, framework or set of intercon-nected pieces or elements. In its literal, physical sense it is a visible and evident edifice, such as a building, a monument, a sculpture, a statue or a bridge. In its more conceptual, abstract sense a structure can be a sys-tem, a network, an organization chart, set of processes or relations. In **organization** and management studies, structure has been a recurrent focus for analysis. This has often gone hand in hand with the concept of process and the interaction between the two. In **normative representa-tions**, structure is commonly seen as something *fixed* (with ontological, object, realist characteristics – see **ontology**, **objectivity**, **reality**) while process is something that takes place in relation to, and around, the set structure. By way of illustration, in **mainstream** commentaries changes in structure are seen as influencing and shaping corporate **cultures**. This view of the role structure tends to be associated with modernistic and positivistic **representations** of organizations (see **modernism** and **positivism**). Structure in this way is frequently seen as linked to a means of exercising managerial control (see **manager** and **managerialism**).

In contrast, more critical approaches discuss structure in a less deter-ministic way (see **determinism**). Rather than being something solid it is seen as a more subjective creation, designed by humans and made sense of in various ways by individuals and groups (see **subjective** and **sense-making**). Processes, formal and informal, official and unofficial all play their role in producing and reproducing structure and processes in a perpetual evolution (see **reproduction**). Within critical perspec-tives, **poststructural** and **postmodern** approaches to organizations have sought to break away from more **mainstream representations** of structure.

Within **normative** and **mainstream** literature, various types of typ-ical structure have been identified and analysed. A traditional form of structure has been the multi-layered hierarchical form (see **hierarchy**). In this model, decisions have to pass up and down through the vari-ous ascending organizational levels. Ranks of **managers** located at the different levels have **authority** to make decisions on particular mat-ters. This style of system exhibits considerable **bureaucracy** and is likely to be seen as rather old-fashioned. On this point it should also be noted that fads, trends and fashion have played a considerable role in the history of organizational structural forms. Further models of struc-ture have included, for example, *divisional* models (where the company is organized into units that deal with different geographical, product or business chain aspects of the overall holding company's business).

Another example is the *matrix* model which encompasses managerial reporting lines both hierarchically and laterally across various business units at the same level (see **hierarchy**). More contemporaneously, neural and virtual-style structures have emerged in organizations (see **emergence**). These have often grown up in relation to information technology advances – especially with regard to the Internet. Equally, contemporary business concepts such as **knowledge** management, learning organizations and 'lean organizations' – often built on practices such as hot-desking, tele-working and home-working – have been important influences on the structure of organizations. These latter forms of organization tend to exhibit fluid, rhizomatic structural characteristics (see **rhizome**).

Key Words:

Authority, Bureaucracy, Control, Culture, Determinism, Knowledge, Manager, Modernism, Objectivity, Ontology, Postmodern, Poststructural, Representation, Rhizome, Sense-making, Subjectivity, Systems.

References

Andrews (2010); Boogaard and Roggeband (2010); Hanlon (2004).

Structuration

'Structuration' is the term accorded to a body of **theory** that aims to reconcile the tensions and relationships between **structure**, action and **agency** (Giddens, 1984). It is a term particularly associated with the British sociologist Anthony Giddens (1938–). Structuration wrestles with the problem of marrying the view that **structure**, as a supposedly fixed entity, produces and cause human actions (see **determinism**). In tandem with this, there is also a need to take strong account of the role of human action in creating and changing **structure**. Nevertheless, an account that uniquely **privileges** human action may not seem to pay due attention to the role of **structures**, regimes and other systematic constraints that may shape and control action. Gidden's work has been an important discussion on these problems and also in relation to concepts such as **agency** and **actor network theory**.

Key Words:

Actor Network Theory, Agency, Privilege.

References

Berends, Boersma and Weggerman (2003); Callahan (2004); Giddens (1984); Lawrence and Phillips (2004); McPhee (2004).

Subjectivity

Subjectivity concerns, among other facets, points of view drawn from an individual, or groups' perspective. It is the product of particular mind(s), imagination(s), **knowledge**(s) and **experiences**. From a **mainstream** and **normative** organizational and managerial perspective, the description of something as 'subjective' is generally likely to be considered as problematic by which is meant that it will be viewed as partial, biased and not based on objective reasoning or rationalism (see **objectivity** and **rationality**). It should be noted that this sense of objectivity is an important element of the underlying modernistic heritage of the **normative** management thinking and associated positivistic methodologies that are commonly employed in research conducted in that vein (see **modernism** and **positivism**).

In contrast, subjectivity is of central importance in **Critical Management Studies** (CMS) accounts. The operation of subjectivity is inextricably linked with **discourse**, **language**, **identity** and the ways in which a person constructs, and makes sense of, **reality**. In turn, this has interplay and consequences with issues of **power** (Foucault, 1961, 1975/1979) (see **sense-making** and **social constructionism**). **Subjectivity** has been a major ongoing strand within the many philosophical theories employed within CMS, including, for example, **postmodernism**, **poststructuralism**, **deconstructionism**, **Critical Theory** and **Critical Realism**. The acknowledgement of subjectivity has led to a wide range of ideas and thinking on alternative ways of looking at **organizations**.

Key Words:

Critical Management Studies, Mainstream, Modernism, Normative, Objectivity, Positivism, Rationality, Sense-Making, Social Constructionism.

References

Bergström and Knights (2006); Böhm and Batta (2010); McCabe (2007); Foucault (1961, 1975/1979).

Surveillance

Surveillance concerns the observation of somebody in a continual, rigorous and close manner. In addition, quite often there is the suggestion or implication of suspicion regarding possible wrongdoing or misdemeanour by the individual(s) concerned. With the increased use of CCTV cameras (not least in the United Kingdom), the introduction of open space working areas and glass office walls, employer monitoring of emails and Internet usage, electronic profiling and tracking, to name but a few of the surveillance interventions that have become commonplace in recent years, it has been suggested that people are watched more than ever. This expansion of surveillance leads to the sense of **panopticon** or an all-seeing eye or observer that monitors individual's every move.

Overall, surveillance (and especially in the contemporary context) is seen as a dominant feature of modernistic environments (see **modernism**). The issues of **power** and control associated with this activity are a source for extensive critique by critical approaches (Sewell and Wilkinson, 1992; Sewell, 1998; Barker, 2005).

Key Words:

Bureaucracy, Modernism, Panopticon, Power.

References

Barker (2005); Kärreman and Alvesson (2009); Sewell (1998); Sewell and Wilkinson (1992).

Symbolism

A symbol is a physical or notional object or concept that stands for or represents (see **representation**) something. Symbolism is the label given to the process or act of using symbols in the process of representing something else. Symbols and symbolism have long played an important role in human history and affairs. Symbols are omnipresent – we find them on products, vehicles, in the media, in schools, colleges, universities and workplaces. Symbols are a central part of personal **identity** embracing, for example, particular tastes, habits, clothing, badges, T-shirts, rings, piercings, club and credit cards – the list is inexhaustible.

Symbols are integral to **discourse**, **language** and the generation of **meaning** stemming from them. Stories and narratives often use symbolism affording people the opportunity to make sense of symbols in a particular context and to be able to represent this so that others may also appreciate and understand (see **sense-making** and **representation**).

In contemporary society, **consumption** and consumerism, whether it is for fashion clothing or for the latest management technique and fad, engages with symbolism extensively. It is indeed difficult to imagine a world without symbols. **Normative** and **mainstream** approaches typically demonstrate a certain degree of awareness and insight into symbols and symbolism and the role they play in corporate life. Illustrations of this might be traditional presentations of marketing and corporate **culture**. However, in contrast, critical approaches are more likely to undertake complex sociological, psychological and philosophical analyses and debates on the multiple possible interpretations, perspectives and behaviours surrounding symbols.

Key Words:

Consumption, Discourse, Identity, Language, Meaning, Representation, Sense-making.

References

Case and Phillipson (2004); Gagliardi (2007); Strati (1998).

Tt

Taylorism

The term 'Taylorism' refers to work patterns that are tightly measured, monitored and controlled with the aim of trying to make them as efficient as possible. The term stems from the name and work of Frederick W. Taylor (1856–1915) and pertains to the approach he adopted to work methods. He sought to move production from a craft basis to a modernistic (see **modernism**) factory-style production line form. The overall approach was named **Scientific Management** pointing at its positivistic, objectivized and modernistic underpinnings and ambitions (see **positivism, modernism, objectivity**).

Taylor's work caused substantial **resistance** from a range of quarters and he was not to realize great success during his lifetime. Nevertheless, the broad concepts underpinning Tayloristic approaches to organization of the workplace have endured and their echoes can still be identified in many contemporary workspaces. Call centres are **organizations** that are often cited as a clear example of Tayloristic practices and atmospheres.

Key Words:

Modernism, Objectivity, Positivism, Resistance, Scientific Management.

References

Peci (2009); Sewell (2005).

Teleology

Teleology is the process of explaining events and phenomena by examining the purposes they serve rather than paying attention to any *claimed* rationale or justification for them (see **rationality**). In other words, teleology is concerned with purpose, end or design. The term 'teleology' (and its adjective teleological) is not a particularly discrete topic or sphere within **Critical Management Studies** (CMS) (such as terms like, by way of example, **resistance** or **surveillance** which can be considered 'subjects' as such within CMS). Rather, it is part of the descriptive vocabulary that is employed to discuss ideas. When the term is employed it is often intended to capture the supposed linear, **boundary**-like categorical finality which modernistic (see **linearity** and **modernism**) **mainstream** and **normative** accounts espouse (see Linstead and Brewis, 2007). This is often juxtaposed against the more subjective, emergent approaches of critical accounts (see **subjectivity**, **emergence**).

Key Words:

Boundaries, Critical Management Studies, Emergence, Linearity, Mainstream, Modernism, Normative, Resistance, Subjectivity, Surveillance.

References

Johnson (2006); Linstead and Brewis (2007); Linstead and Pullen (2006).

Temporal

Temporal relates to time. When the term 'temporal' is employed it is pointing at some chronological or time-related aspect of what is being discussed. It would perhaps be reasonable to ask the question why not simply use the word 'time'. This is perfectly acceptable, but temporal offers commentators the opportunity to allude to a more abstract and conceptual dimension of time by using this specialist **language** or **discourse**. Temporal is occasionally used in conjunction with, or in relation to, **spatial** (pertaining to *space* dimensions) to signal the time–space (ontological) dimensions of subjects (see Hancock, 2006) (see ontology).

Key Words:

Discourse, Language.

References

Fairhurst (2004); Hancock (2006).

Theory

A theory is an explanation and a system or collection of ideas that work together to elaborate and illustrate an issue or problem. Theories are produced or emerge from different patterns of philosophical thought. This means that, just as various philosophies have differing epistemological (ways that **knowledge** is made) and ontological (attitudes to what constitutes **reality**), so do the theories that constitute them or that are subsequently produced by them (see **epistemology** and **ontology**). Theories are produced by both inductive and deductive-style (see **inductivism**, **deductivism**) approaches but the characteristics, commitments and principles of those theories are likely to differ considerably.

For **Critical Management Studies** (CMS), the main commitments of theory building tend broadly to follow inductive, interpretivistic (see **interpretivism**) approaches that envisage an important role for **subjectivity**. Although it is of course difficult to generalize, this contrasts sharply with the **modernistic deductivist**, **positivistic**-style (studies that are often conducted in **mainstream** and **normative** texts (see **deductivism** and **positivism**).

Key Words:

Deductivism, Epistemology, Inductivism, Interpretivism, Ontology, Reality, Subjectivity.

References

Clegg, Kornberger and Pitsis (2008); Tadajewski (2009a).

Trust

'Trust' is an everyday word **meaning** something or someone that can be relied on to behave in a particular way or to have certain traits and characteristics. In recent decades, trust has become a widely examined aspect of **organization** and management. This has taken place in tandem with a rise in interest in related areas such as **ethics**, conduct and corporate governance. Trust is frequently viewed as a necessary condition and even prerequisite for commercial relations and organizational life. Nevertheless, it is a complex phenomenon and it is evident that variable trust patterns and types of trust are at play in the corporate and wider social sphere (see Adler, 2005a, 2005b).

Key Words:

Conduct, Corporate Governance, Ethics.

References

Adler (2005a, 2005b); Amalya and Montgomery (2001); Hanlon (2004).

Truth

Truth concerns what is considered to be true or a 'fact'. In other words, this might be equivalent to what is 'accurate', 'good', 'right', 'valid' and so on and so forth. For deductive approaches to **sense-making**, truth tends to be seen as an objective fact – things are either right or wrong and they fall into a given category or not (see **deductivism** and **objectivity**). In other words, they are true and valid for that particular belief system, **theory**, classification or categorization. Critiques employing more inductive and subjective views of truth, such as critical approaches, see truth as being less categorical (see **inductivism** and **subjectivity**). Truth is a view, a perspective or a point of view. Truth is made or constructed (or not) based on the given (or shifting) contexts and philosophical perspectives adhered to. For example, somebody who makes sense of the world using a deductive, positivistic methodology would not see notions of truth in the same manner that a person employing a postmodern or poststructuralist perspective would (see **deductivism**, **positivism**, **postmodernism** and **poststructuralism**).

Key Words:

Positivism, Postmodernism, Sense-making.

References

Al-Amoudi (2007); Arthur (2003); Llewellyn and Harrison (2007).

Uu

Unitary

In organizations with unitary patterns of working it is anticipated that everyone will believe, follow and pull in the same direction for a common set of organizational aims and objectives. The key point to note in unitary settings is that senior managers are the organizational members allotted the task of setting objectives and everybody else, as contracted employees, is expected to adhere and follow. In unitary environments, dissenting **voices** are not always welcome and this type of behaviour is often seen as dysfunctional and needing to be controlled. **Managers** have the **authority** to manage and govern the firm and hence, inherently and implicitly, the right to exercise the **power** associated with that **authority**. It can be imagined that hierarchies (see **hierarchy**) and the belief that every employee knows and adheres to their role, duties and responsibilities is very important in unitary espousing organizations. Simply stated in a unitary organization all the employees should be 'singing from the same hymn sheet'.

While in everyday working life unitary forms of organization and management are often considered **normative** or idealized ways of operating an organization, they are often contrasted with pluralistic forms (where many **voices** are likely to be openly active in the **organization** – see **pluralism**). Unitary-styled organizations can appear as closed, controlling and even oppressive to alternative viewpoints of employees (Noon and Blyton, 2006). Equally, in a unitary environment the notion of alternative **power** centres such as departmental bastions, manager cliques and so on does not, at least officially, have a place in organization.

Moreover, it can also be imagined that some managers may publically talk the **rhetoric** of the **pluralistic** nature of the firm but in reality the firm is run on a strong unitary basis. The fact that alternative **voices** to an imposed unitary view are not desirable does not mean that these, and commensurate **resistance**, will not exist. Critical approaches typically challenge the **reality** and validity of unitary **representations** of **organizations** and see pluralistic-style **organizations** as more relevant and useful way in which to appreciate this phenomenon.

Key Words:

Authority, Hierarchy, Pluralistic, Power, Resistance, Voice.

References

Learmouth (2009); Noon and Blyton (2006); Sturdy, Clark, Fincham and Handley (2009); Thomas and Davies (2005).

Utopian (also dystopias and heterotopias)

The idea of utopia is one of an ideal situation. For certain commentators and practitioners, the contemporary dominance (i.e. **hegemony**) of globalized markets, capital accompanied by widespread **managerialism**, **consumption** and consumerism may seem to represent progression to a utopian state of affairs. For others, a world having these facets may be far from perfect or utopian. Rather it is a *dystopia* or perfectly dysfunctional situation.

Critical Management Studies (CMS) aims, among other things, to analyse and critique why hegemonic state of affairs are far from ideal (see **hegemony**). In so doing, it does not intend to replace one dystopia with another one but rather to point up some of the effects and situations of the *status quo*. This might be achieved for example through (micro-) **emancipations** of individuals and groups whose **voice** is marginalized or oppressed (Parker, 2002a, 2002b; Parker, Fournier and Reedy, 2007).

In contrast to utopia, which alludes to physical possible ideal, heterotopias offer a space of nothingness which do not seek to be perfect or dominant (see **hegemony**) (Foucault, 1967/1984). In **spatial** terms, they are fleeting and ephemeral, like the reflection in a mirror or the moment of a telephone call. Foucault suggested that heterotopias are essential for life to be able to operate because 'nothingness' constitutes spaces where acts such as repression, oppression and totalitarianism cannot reach.

However, CMS cannot and would not suggest that it offers a utopian substitute or replacement for **mainstream managerialism**. In its turn, CMS has been charged with being anti-management, anti-profit, anti-corporate and non-**performativity**-focused. It finds its alternative propositions often accused (by CMS as much as **normative** adherents) as vague, weak and nebulous guides for employees and **managers** to enact, all too frequently relying on discursive (see **discourse**) and linguistic turns. The concept of utopianism is not one extensively discussed or addressed in CMS texts; however, it is a thought-provoking and challenging one for **mainstream** and CMS commentators alike.

Key Words:

Consumerism, Dystopia, Emancipation Hegemony, Managerialism.

References

Foucault (1967/1984); Parker (2002a, 2002b); Parker, Fournier and Reedy (2007).

Vv Ww Xx Yy Zz

Violence

Violence is the use of strong and intense force. This is typically used against **others** but could consist of violence against the self (i.e. as in self-harm). Violence often causes hurt, damage or degradation and is, tragically, a frequent feature of human existence (Arendt, 1970). Violence is commonly thought of as taking place in certain domains, such as for example, the global geo-political arena where nations go to war, conduct conflicts, border skirmishes, invasions and so on and so forth (see **politics**). Equally, in the civil arena violence is a possible risk in daily life including the risk of being mugged, aggressed or assaulted. For some people, living in particularly harrowing circumstances (for example, severely disadvantaged individuals, prison inmates etc.) this risk may be more apparent.

Critically styled accounts of organizations have taken a gradual and increasing interest in violence in organizational and managerial contexts. This is still not an extensively developed domain, however, this may be due, in part, to the difficult, uncomfortable, embarrassing and distressing nature of the phenomenon (Burrell, 1997).

In everyday work settings, violence may of course be physical where, for example, a person bodily attacks or hits another and this may invoke criminal prosecution or disciplinary procedures. However, commentators have also drawn attention to the myriad ways in which (soft) violence may occur. Violence can be perceived as taking place through, for instance, character assassination, redundancy, denial of **voice** to, bullying or harassment of particular individuals or groups (Stein, 2001; Sims, 2003). This form of **culture** can be part of any workplace but may be particularly (although not necessarily) associated with managerialist-style approaches to managing people and work (see managerialism). Moreover, postcolonial studies is one particular area where corporate and organizational 'aggression' has caused violence and negative **experiences** in relation to territorial occupation and cultural imposition or occlusion of national **identity** (see **postcolonialism**).

Key Words:

Aggression, Experience, Postcolonialism, Redundancy, Voice.

References

Arendt (1970); Burrell (1997); Parker (2008); Robinson and Kerr (2009); Sims (2003); Stein (2001).

Voice

The notion of voice concerns the **power**, moment and **reality** of being able to express views, influence events and participate in decision-making and actions. Voice is a core aspect of **identity** and relates to individuals, groups of people and various sections of society – indeed everyone in principle has a voice. Voice is an important concept in critical approaches. An illustration of how voice might not be allowed to operate so well is apparent in, for example, **organizations** that believe they operate on a **unitary** basis (where everyone is supposed to pulling in the same direction and 'singing from the same hymn sheet'). Unitary contrasts with pluralistic organizations (where there are multiple views and perspectives in operation) (see **pluralism**). **Organizations** often appear *prima facie* unitary in that senior management and directors seek to promote and introduce one particular set of visions (or voice) however this does not mean that multifarious or plural opinions exist.

The presence of voice(s) also raises issues of **appropriation** or **silencing** of voice(s). **Appropriation** occurs where, either deliberately or inadvertently, a person or group speaks on behalf of another and thereby denies them the opportunity to express himself or herself. When this occurs the person's voice is said to have been 'appropriated' and he or she is said to have been 'silenced'. It is frequently considered an important role of academics to speak out on behalf of those who may have been silenced (see Parker, 1995; Wray-Bliss, 2004).

Key Words:

Pluralistic, Power, Silence, Unitary.

References

Bell and Taylor (2004); Fletcher and Watson (2007); Kim, MacDuffie and Pil (2010); Parker (1995); Simpson and Lewis (2005); Wray-Bliss (2004).

Weltanschauung (world view)

Weltanschauung is a German word from philosophy indicating the particular holistic view of, or approach to, the world that a given person has developed and according to which he or she sees the world and conducts his or her life. The formation of a person's Weltanschauung is an evolutionary process and may transform and change over time as the person is exposed to different **experiences**.

Key Words:

Experience, Subjectivity.

References

Bell and Taylor (2004); Tadajewski (2009a).

References

Ackroyd, S. and Fleetwood, S. (2001) *Realist Perspectives on Organization and Management*, London, Routledge.

Ackroyd, S. and Thompson, P. (1999) *Organizational Misbehaviour*, London, Sage Publications.

Adler, P. (2005a) 'Market, hierarchy and trust' in Grey, C. and Willmott, H. (eds) *Critical Management Studies: A Reader*, Oxford, Oxford University Press.

Adler, P. (2005b) 'The evolving object of software development', *Organization*, 12(3): 401–435.

Adler, P. (2008) 'CMS: Resist the three complacencies', *Organization*, 15(6): 925–926.

Adler, P. (2009) *The Oxford Handbook of Sociology and Organization Studies*, Oxford, Oxford University Press.

Adler, P., Forbes, L. and Willmott, H. (2007) 'Critical management studies', *The Academy of Management Annals*, December, 1: 119–179.

Adorno, T. (1997) *Aesthetic Theory*, Minneapolis, University of Minnesota Press.

Adorno, T., Frenkel-Brunswick, E., Levinson, D. and Sandford, N. (1950) *The Authoritarian Personality*, New York, Harper and Row.

Al-Amoudi, I. (2007) 'Redrawing Foucault's social ontology', *Organization*, 14(4): 543–563.

Alcadipani, R. and Hassard, J. (2010) 'Actor network theory, organizations and critique: Towards a politics or organizing', *Organization*, 14(4): 419–435.

Allard-Poesi, F. (2005) 'The paradox of sensemaking in organizational analysis', *Organization*, 12(2): 169–196.

Alvarez, J.-L., Mazza, C. and Pedersen, J. and Svejenova, S. (2005) 'Shielding idiosyncrasy from isomorphic pressures: Towards optimal distinctiveness in European filmmaking', *Organization*, 12(6): 863–888.

Alvesson, M. (2002) *Understanding Organizational Culture*, London, Sage Publications.

Alvesson, M. and Billing, Y. (2009) *Understanding Gender and Organizations*, London, Sage Publications.

Alvesson, M. and Deetz, S. (1999) *Doing Critical Management Research*, London, Sage Publications.

Alvesson, M. and Deetz, S. (2005) 'Critical theory and postmodernism' in Grey, C. and Willmott, H. (eds) *Critical Management Studies: A Reader*, Oxford, Oxford University Press.

Alvesson, M. and Kärreman, D. (2000) 'Varieties of discourse: On the study of organizations through discourse analysis', *Human Relations*, 53(9): 1125–1149.

Alvesson, M. and Robertson, M. (2006) 'The brightest and the best: The role of elite identity in knowledge intensive companies', *Organization*, 13(2): 195–224.

Alvesson, M. and Sköldberg, K. (2009) *Reflexive Methodology, New Vistas in Qualitative Research*, London, Sage Publications.

Alvesson, M. and Spicer, A. (2010) *Understanding Leadership in the Real World: Metaphors We Lead By*, London, Routledge.

Alvesson, M. and Willmott, H. (1992) *Critical Management Studies*, London, Sage Publications.

Alvesson, M. and Willmott, H. (1996) *Making Sense of Management: A Critical Introduction*, London, Sage Publications.

Alvesson, M., Bridgeman, T. and Willmott, H. (2009) *The Oxford Handbook of Critical Management Studies*, Oxford, Oxford University Press.

Amalya, O. and Montgomery, K. (2001) 'A system cybernetic approach to the dynamics of individual- and organizational-level trust', *Human Relations*, 54(8): 1045–1063.

Anderson, G. (2008) 'Mapping academic resistance in the managerial university', *Organization*, 15(2): 251–270.

Andrews, R. (2010) 'Organizational social capital, structure and performance', *Human Relations*, 63(5): 583–608.

Arendt, H. (1970) *On Violence*, New York, Harcourt.

Armitage, J. (ed.) (2002) *Paul Virilio: From Modernism to Hypermodernism and Beyond*, London, Sage Publications.

Armitage, J. and Roberts, J. (2002) *Living with Cyberspace: Technology & Society in the 21st Century*, London, Continuum.

Arthur, A. (2003) 'A utility theory of "Truth"', *Organization*, 10(2): 205–221.

Atkin, I., Hassard, J. and Cox, J. (2007) 'Excess and mimesis in organization theory: Emancipation from within?', *Culture and Organization*, 13: 145–156.

Badham, R., Garrety, K., Morrigan, V. and Zanko, M. (2003) 'Designer deviance: Enterprise and deviance in culture change programmes', *Organization*, 10(4): 707–730.

Ball, A. and Brewis, J. (2008) 'Guest editorial – gender counts: "work", "life" and identity in accounting practice and education', *Pacific Accounting Review*, 20(2): 85–93.

Ball, K. (2005) 'Organization, surveillance and the body: Towards a politics of resistance', *Organization*, 12(1): 89–108.

Banerjee, B. and Linstead, S. (2004) 'Masking subversion: Neo-colonial embeddedness in anthropological accounts of indigenous management', *Human Relations*, 57(2): 221–247.

Barker, J. (2005) 'Tightening the iron cage: Concertive control in self-managing teams' in Grey, C. and Willmott, H. (eds) *Critical Management Studies: A Reader*, Oxford, Oxford university Press.

Baudrillard, J. (1975) *The Mirror of Production*, St. Louis, Telos Press.

Baudrillard, J. (1983) *Simulations*, New York, Semiotext(e).

Baudrillard, J. (1988) 'Simulacra and simulations' in Poster, M. (ed.) *Jean Baudrillard: Selected Writings*, Cambridge, Polity Press.

Bauman, Z. (1989) *Modernity and the Holocaust*, Cambridge, Polity Press.

Bell, E. and Taylor, S. (2003) 'The elevation of work: Pastoral power and the new age work ethic', *Organization*, 10(2): 329–349.

Bell, E. and Taylor, S. (2004) 'From outward bound to inward bound: The prophetic voices and discursive practices of spiritual management development', *Human Relations*, 57(4): 439–466.

Berends, H., Boersma, K. and Weggerman, M. (2003) 'The structuration of organizational learning', *Human Relations*, 56(9): 1035–1056.

Berger, P. and Luckmann, T. (1966) *The Social Construction of Reality: A Treatise in the Sociology of Knowledge*, London, Penguin.

Bergström, O. and Knights, D. (2006) 'Organizational discourse and subjectivity: Subjectification during processes of recruitment', *Human Relations*, 59(3): 351–377.

Best, S. and Kellner, D. (1991) *Postmodern Theory: Critical Interrogations*, New York, Guildford Press.

Bhaskar, R. (1989) *The Possibility of Naturalism*, Hemel Hempstead, Harvester Wheatsheaf.

Blaug, R. (1999) 'The tyranny of the visible: Problems in the evaluation of anti-institutional radicalism', *Organization*, 6(1): 33–56.

Blomberg, J. (2009) 'Gendering finance: Masculinities and hierarchies at the Stockholm stock exchange', *Organization*, 16(2): 203–225.

Böhm, S. (2006) *Repositioning Organization Theory*, Basingstoke, Palgrave Macmillan.

Böhm, S. and Batta, A. (2010) 'Just doing it: Enjoying commodity of fetishism with Lacan', *Organization*, May 17(3): 345–361.

Boje, D. (1995) 'Stories of the storytelling organization: A postmodern analysis of Disney as "Tamara-land"', *Academy of Management Journal*, 38(4): 997–1035.

Boje, D. (2008) *Storytelling Organizations*, London, Sage Publications.

Bolton, S. and Boyd, C. (2003) 'Trolley dolly or skilled emotion manager? Moving on from Hochschild's emotional labour', *Work, Employment and Society*, 17(2): 289–308.

Bolton, S. and Houlihan, M. (2009) *Work Matters: Critical Reflections on Contemporary Work*, Basingstoke, Palgrave Macmillan.

Boogaard, B. and Roggeband, C. (2010) 'Paradoxes of intersectionality: Theorizing inequality in Dutch Police force through structure and agency', *Organization*, 17(1): 53–75.

Borch, C. (2010) 'Organizational atmospheres: Focus, affect and architecture', *Organization*, March 17(2): 223–241.

Bourdieu, P. (1984) *Distinction: A Social Critique of the Judgement of Taste*, London, Routledge.

Bowen, F. and Blackmon, K. (2003) 'Spirals of silence: The dynamic effects of diversity on organizational voice', *Journal of Management Studies*, September 40(6): 1393–1417.

Bowring, M.A. and Brewis, J. (2009) 'Truth and consequences: Managing lesbian and gay identity in the Canadian workplace', *Equal Opportunities International*, 28(5): 361–377.

Braverman, H. (1974) *Labor and Monopoly Capital*, The Degradation of Work in the Twentieth Century, New York, Monthly Review Press.

Brewis, J. and Linstead, S. (2009) 'Gender and management' in Linstead, S., Fulop, L. and Lilley, S. (eds) *Management and Organization: A Critical Text*, Basingtoke, Palgrave Macmillan, pp. 89–146.

Brown, A., Gabriel, Y. and Gherardi, S. (2009) 'Storytelling and change: An unfolding story', *Organization*, 16(3): 323–333.

Brown, A., Stacey, P. and Nandhakumar, J. (2008) 'Making sense of sensemaking narratives', *Human Relations*, 61(8): 1035–1062.

Bryman, A. (2004) *The Disneyization of Society*, London, Sage Publications.

Bryman, A. and Bell, E. (2007) *Business Research Methods*, Oxford, Oxford University Press.

Buchanan, D. and Badham, R. (2009) *Power, Politics and Organizational Change: Winning the Turf Game*, London, Sage Publications.

Burrell, G. (1997) *Pandemonium: Towards a Retro-Organizational Theory*, London, Sage Publications.

Burrell, G. and Morgan, G. (1979) *Sociological Paradigms and Organizational Analysis*, Oxford, Heinemann Educational Ltd.

Burton, D. (2001) 'Critical marketing theory: The blueprint?' *European Journal of Marketing*, 35(5/6): 722–743.

Butler, J., Laclau, E. and Žižek, S. (2000) *Contingency Hegemony, Universality: Contemporary Dialogues on the Left*, London, Verso.

Caldwell, R. (2007) 'Agency and change: Re-evaluating Foucault's legacy', *Organization*, 14(6): 769–791.

Callahan, J. (2004) 'Reversing a conspicuous absence: Mindful inclusion of emotion in structuration theory', *Human Relations*, 57(11): 1427–1448.

Carter, C. and Muller, F. (2002) 'The "long march" of the management modernisers: Ritual, rhetoric and rationality', *Human Relations*, 55(11): 1325–1354.

Carter, J. and Rayner, M. (1996) 'The curious case of post-Fordism and welfare', *Journal of Social Policy*, 25: 347–367.

Carter, P. and Jackson, N. (2006) *Rethinking Organizational Behaviour: A Poststructuralist Approach*, Harlow, Pearson Education Ltd.

Carey, M. (2009) ' "It's a bit like being a robot or working in a factory": Does Braverman help explain the experiences of state social workers since 1971?', *Organization*, 16(4): 505–527.

Case, P. and Phillipson, G. (2004) 'Astrology, alchemy and retro-organization theory, an astro-genealogical critique of the Myers–Briggs type indicator', *Organization*, 11(4): 473–495.

Casey, C. (2004) 'Bureaucracy re-enchanted? Spirit, experts and authority in organizations', 11(1): 59–79.

Chia, R. (1996) *Organizational Analysis as Deconstructive Practice*, Berlin, Walter de Gruyter and Co.

Clark, P. (2000) *Organizations in Action: Competition Between Contexts*, London, Routledge.

Clarke, J., Gerwitz, S. and McLaughlin, E. (2000) *New Managerialism, New Welfare*, London, Sage Publications/Open University Press.

Clegg, S. and Haugaard, M. (2009) *The Sage Handbook of Power*, London, Sage Publications.

Clegg, S., Courpasson, D. and Phillips, N. (2006) *Power and Organizations*, London, Sage Publications.

Clegg, S., Kornberger, M. and Pitsis, T. (2008) *Managing and Organizations: An Introduction to Theory and Practice*, London, Sage Publications.

Clegg, S., Kornberger, M. and Rhodes, C. (2005) 'Learning/becoming/organizing', *Organization*, 12(2): 147–167.

Clegg, S., Kornberger, M., Carter, C. and Rhodes, C. (2006) 'For management', *Management Learning*, 37(1): 7–27.

Coleman, J.S. (1988) 'Social capital in the creation of human capital', *American Journal of Sociology*, 94: S95–S120.

Collins, D. (2004) 'The machinations of change: BEEPEEARR, debunking and the in-between', *Organization*, 11(5): 671–688.

Collinson, D. (1994) 'Strategies of resistance: Power, knowledge and subjectivity in the workplace' in Jermier, J., Knights, D. and Nord, W. (eds) *Resistance and Power in Organizations*, New York, Routledge, pp. 25–68.

Contu, A. and Willmott, H. (2005) 'You spin me round: The realist turn in organization and management studies', *Journal of Management Studies*, 42: 1622–1645.

Contu, A., Driver, M. and Jones, C. (2010) 'Jacques Lacan and organization studies', special issue of *Organization*, 17(3): 307–315.

Cooke, B. (1999) 'Writing the left out of management theory: The historiography of the management of change', *Organization*, 6: 81–105.

Cooke, B. (2004) 'The managing of the (Third) world', *Organization*, 11(5): 603–629.

Cooke, B. (2008) 'If critical management studies is your problem...', *Organization*, 15(6): 912–914.

Cooper, B. (1989) 'Modernism, postmodernism and organizational analysis 3: The contribution of Jacques Derrida', *Organization Studies*, 10(4): 479–502.

Cooper, R. (2010) 'The generalized social body: Distance and technology', *Organization*, 17(2): 242–256.

Corbett, M. (1995) 'Celluloid projections: Images of technology and organizational futures in contemporary science fiction film', *Organization*, 2(3/4): 467–488.

Corona, V. and Godart, F. (2010) 'Network-domains in combat and fashion organizations', *Organization*, 17(2): 283–304.

Courpasson, D. and Clegg, S. (2006) 'Dissolving the iron cages?: Tocqueville, Michels, bureaucracy and the perpetuation of elite power', *Organization*, 13(3): 319–343.

Cremin, C. (2010) 'Never employable enough: The (im)possibility of satisfying the boss' desire', *Organization*, 17(2): 131–149.

Crozier, M. (1964) *The Bureaucratic Phenomenon*, London, Tavistock.

Cummings, S. (2002) *ReCreating Strategy*, London, Sage Publications.

Czarniawska, B. (1998) *A Narrative Approach to Organization Studies*, London, Sage Publications.

Czarniawska, B. (2004) *Narratives in Social Science Research*, London, Sage Publications.

Czarniawska, B. and Hopfl, H. (2002) *The Production and Maintenance of Inequalities in Work Organizations*, London, Routledge.

Deal, T. and Kennedy, A. (1982) *Corporate Cultures: The Rites and Rituals of Corporate Life*, Harmondsworth, Penguin Books.

De Beauvoir, S. (1949) *Le Deuxième Sexe*, Paris, Gallimard.

De Clerq, D. and Voronov, M. (2009) 'The role of domination in newcomers' legitimation as entrepreneurs', *Organization*, 16(6): 799–827.

Deleuze, G. and Guattari, F. (1987) *A Thousand Plateaus: Capitalism and Schizophrenia*, Minneapolis, University of Minnesota Press.

Dent, M. (2003) 'Managing doctors and saving a hospital: Irony, rhetoric and actor networks', *Organization*, 10(1): 107–127.

Denzin, N. and Lincoln, Y. (2008) *The Landscape of Qualitative Research*, London, Sage Publications.

Dereli, C. and Stokes, P. (2007) 'Reconceptualising modernity for management studies: Exploring the tension between the scientific and the spiritual in the age of modernism', *Philosophy of Management*, 6(2): 131–139.

Derrida, J. (1976) *Of Grammatology*, Baltimore and London, John Hopkins University Press.

Deuze, M. (2006) 'Participation, remediation, bricolage: Considering principal components of a digital culture', *The Information Society*, 22(2): 63–75.

Dey, P. and Steyaert, C. (2007) 'The Troubadours of knowledge: Passion and invention in management education', *Organization*, 14(3): 437–461.

Di Maggio, P. and Powell, W. (2002) 'The iron cage revisited: Institutional isomorphism and collective rationality in organizational fields' in Clegg, S. (ed.) *Central Currents in Organizational Studies: Frameworks and Applications Vol 3.*, London, Sage Publications, pp. 324–362.

Drucker, Peter (1954) *The Practice of Management*, London, Heron Books.

Du Gay, P. (1995) *Consumption and Identity at Work*, London, Sage Publications.

Du Gay, P. (2000a) *In Praise of Bureaucracy: Weber – Organization – Ethics*, London, Sage Publications.

Du Gay, P. (2000b) *The Values of Bureaucracy*, Oxford, Oxford University Press.

Du Gay, P. and Elliott, A. (2008) *Identity in Question*, London, Sage Publications.

Du Gay, P., Evans, J. and Redman, P. (2000) *Identity: A Reader*, London, Sage Publications.

Eastmond, M. (2007) 'Stories as lived experience: Narratives in forced migration research', *Journal of Refugee Studies*, 20(2): 248–264.

Eden, C. (1987) 'Problem Solving or Problem Finishing?' in Jackson, M.C. and Keys, P. (eds) *New Directions in Management Science*, Hants, Gower, pp. 97–107.

Ellis, N. (2008) 'What the hell is that: The representation of professional service markets in The Simpsons', *Organization*, 15(5): 705–723.

Elmes, M. and Frame, B. (2008) 'Into hot air: A critical perspective on Everest', *Human Relations*, 61(2): 213–241.

Essers, C. (2009) 'Reflections on the narrative approach: Dilemmas of power, emotions and social location while constructing life-stories', *Organization*, 16(2): 163–181.

Fairclough, N. (2005) 'Discourse analysis in organization studies: The case for critical realism', *Organization Studies*, 26(6): 915–939.

Fairclough, N. (2010) (2nd edn) *Critical Discourse Analysis: The Critical Study of Language*, Harlow, Pearson Education Ltd.

Fairhurst, G. (2004) 'Textuality and agency in interaction analysis', *Organization*, 11(3): 335–353.

Fay, E. (2008) 'Derision and management', *Organization*, 15(6): 831–850.

Fayol, H. (1949) *General and Industrial Management*, London, Pitman.

Fineman, S. (1993) *Emotion in Organizations*, London, Sage Publications.

Fineman, S. (2003) *Understanding Emotion at Work*, London, Sage Publications.

Fineman, S. (2007) *The Emotional Organization: Passions and Power*, Oxford, Wiley-Blackwell.

Fineman, S., Gabriel, Y. and Sims, D. (2009) *Organizing and Organizations*, London, Sage Publications.

——. (2010) *Organizing and Organizations*, London, Sage Publications.

Finn, R. (2008) 'The language of teamwork: Reproducing professional divisions in the operating theatre', *Human Relations*, 61(1): 103–130.

Fleetwood, S. (2005) 'The ontology of organization and management studies: A critical realist approach', *Organization*, 12(2): 197–222.

Fleetwood, S. and Ackroyd, S. (2004) *Critical Realist Applications in Organization and Management Studies*, London, Routledge.

Fleming, P. (2001) 'Beyond the panopticon', *Ephemera*, 1(2): 190–194.

Fleming, P. (2007) 'Sexuality, power and resistance in the workplace', *Organization Studies*, 28(2): 239–256.

Fleming, P. and Spicer, A. (2004) ' "You can check out anytime, but you can never leave": Spatial boundaries in a high commitment organization', *Human Relations*, 57(1): 75–94.

Fleming, P. and Spicer, A. (2007) *Contesting the Corporation: Struggle, Power and Resistance in Organizations*, Cambridge, Cambridge University Press.

Fletcher, D. and Watson, T. (2007) 'Voice, silence and the business of construction: Loud and quiet voices in the construction of personal, organizational and social realities', *Organization*, 14(2): 155–174.

Foucault, M. (1961) *Madness and Civilization: A History of Insanity in the Age of Reason*, New York, Vintage Books.

Foucault, M. (1963) *The Birth of the Clinic: An Archeology of Medical Perception*, London, Penguin.

Foucault, M. (1975/1979) *Discipline and Punish*, London, Penguin.

Foucault, M. (1976) *The History of Sexuality: Vol 1 – The Will to Pleasure*, London, Penguin.

Foucault, M. (1977) *Madness and Civilisation*, London, Tavistock.

Foucault, M. Dits et écrits (1984) *Des espaces autres* (conférence au Cercle d'études architecturales, 14 mars 1967), in *Architecture, Mouvement, Continuité*, n°5, octobre, pp. 46–49.

Foucault, M. (1984a) *The History of Sexuality: Vol II The Use of Pleasure*, London, Penguin.

Foucault, M. (1984b) *The History of Sexuality: Vol III The Care of the Self*, London, Penguin.

Fournier, V. and Grey, C. (2000) 'At the critical moment: Conditions and prospects for critical management studies', *Human Relations*, 50(4): 363–391.

Frenkel, M. (2005) 'The politics of translation: How state-level political relations affect the cross-national travel of management ideas', *Organization*, 12(2): 275–301.

Friedland, R. (2009) 'The endless fields of Pierre Bourdieu', *Organization*, 16(6): 887–917.

Friedman, M. (1970) 'The social responsibility of business is to increase its profits', *New York Times Magazine*, 13 September, 32–33.

Gabriel, Y. (2000) *Storytelling in Organizations: Facts, Fictions and Fantasies*, Oxford, Oxford University Press.

Gabriel, Y. (2002) 'Essai: On paragrammatic uses of organizational theory – A provocation', *Organization Studies*, 23(1): 133–151.

Gabriel, Y. (2004) *Myths, Stories and Organizations: Pre-Modern Narratives for Our Times*, Oxford, Oxford University Press.

Gabriel, Y. (2005) 'Glass cages and glass palaces: Images of organization in image-conscious times', *Organization*, 12(1): 9–27.

Gabriel, Y. and Willman, P. (2004) 'The journal swap line: Boundaries or integration', *Human Relations*, 57: 7–8.

Gagliardi, P. (2007) 'The collective repression of "pathos" in organization studies', *Organization*, 14(3): 331–338.

Giddens, A. (1979) *Central Problems in Social Theory: Action, Structure and Contradiction in Social Analysis*, London, Palgrave Macmillan.

Giddens, A. (1984) *The Constitution of Society: Outline of a Theory of Structuration*, Cambridge, Polity Press.

Gill, R. (2006) 'Global feminism: Trend in the literature' (review essay), *Organization*, 13(4): 589–598.

Goffman, I. (1959) *The Presentation of Self in Everyday Life*, New York, Anchor Books.

Golsorkhi, D., Leca, B., Lounsbury, M. and Ramirez, C. (2009) 'Analysing, accounting for and unmasking domination: On our role as scholars of practice, practitioners of social sciences and public intellectuals', *Organization*, 16(6): 779–797.

Gouldner, A. (1954) *Patterns of Industrial Bureaucracy*, New York, Free Press.

Grant, D., Hardy, C., Oswick, C. and Putnam, L. (2004) *The Sage Handbook of Organizational Discourse*, London, Sage Publications.

Greenwood, R., Olivier, C., Suddaby, R. and Sahlin-Andersson, K. (2008) *The Sage Handbook of Organizational Institutionalism*, London, Sage Publications.

Greer, G. (1970) *The Female Eunuch*, London, Granada.

Grey, C. (2008) *A Very Short, Fairly Interesting and Reasonably Cheap Book About Studying Organizations*, London, Sage Publications.

Grey, C. (2009) 'Security studies and organization studies: Parallels and possibilities', *Organization*, 17(2): 199–222.

Grey, C. and Willmott, H. (2005) *Critical Management Studies: A Reader*, Oxford, Oxford University Press.

Grint, K. (2005) 'Problems, problems, problems: The social construction of "leadership"', *Human Relations*, 58(11): 1467–1494.

Gustafson, C., Rehn, A. and Skold, D. (2005) *Excess and Organization: Proceedings of SCOS XXIII: Stockholm 2005*, Department of Industrial Management and Organization, The Royal Institute of Technology, Stockholm, Sweden.

Halsall, R. (2008) 'Intercultural mergers and acquisitions as "Legitimacy Cases" of models of capitalism: A UK–German case study', *Organization*, 15(6): 787–809.

Hancock, P. (2005) 'Uncovering the semiotic in organizational aesthetics', *Organization,* 12(1): 29–50.

Hancock, P. (2006) 'The spatial and temporal mediation of social change', *Journal of Organizational Change Management,* 19(5): 619–639.

Hanlon, G. (2004) 'Institutional forms and organizational structures: Homology, trust and reputational capital in professional service firms', *Organization,* 11(2): 186–210.

Hardy, C. (2004) 'Scaling up and bearing down in discourse analysis: Questions regarding textual agencies and their content', *Organization,* 11(3): 415–425.

Haski-Leventhal, D. and Bargal, D. (2008) 'The volunteer stages and transitions model: Organizational socialization of volunteers', *Human Relations,* 61(1): 67–102.

Hassard, J., Holliday, R. and Willmott, H. (2000) *Body and Organization,* London, Sage Publications.

Hatch, M.J. and Rubin, J. (2006) 'The hermeneutics of branding', *Journal of Brand Management,* 14, 40–59.

Hayes, N. and Walsham, G. (2000) 'Competing interpretations of computer-supported cooperative work in organizational contexts', *Organization,* 7(1): 49–67.

Hearn, J. (1996) 'Deconstructing the dominant: Making the one(s) the other(s)', *Organization,* 3: 683–722.

Hellström, T. (2004) 'Innovation as social action', *Organization,* 11(5): 631–649.

Heracleous, L. (2004) 'Boundaries in the study of organization', *Human Relations,* 57: 95–103.

Hernes, T. (2004) 'Studying composite boundaries: A framework of analysis', *Human Relations,* 57: 9–29.

Higgins, W. and Tamm-Hallström, K. (2007) 'Standardization, globalization and rationalities of government', *Organization,* 14(5): 685–704.

Hjorth, D. and Pelzer, P. (2007) 'The fate of Phaeton: Baroque art for management's sake?', *Organization,* 14(6): 869–886.

Hochschild, A. (1983) *The Managed Heart: Commercialization of Human Feeling,* Berkeley/Los Angeles, University of California Press.

Hodge, B. and Coronado, G. (2006) 'Mexico Inc?: Discourse analysis and the triumph of managerialism', *Organization,* 13(4): 529–547.

Hodgson, D. (2005) ' "Putting on a professional performance": Performativity, subversion and project management', *Organization,* 12(1): 51–68.

Hopfl, H. (2004) 'Julia Kristeva' in Linstead, S. (ed.) *Organization Theory and Postmodern Thought,* London, Sage, pp. 88–104.

Hotho, S. and Pollard, D. (2007) 'Management as negotiation at the interface: Moving beyond the critical-practice impasse', *Organization,* 14(4): 583–603.

House, D. (2001) 'Agent of changelessness: The development and commodification of biotechnology', *Organization,* 8(2): 251–258.

Humphreys, M., Brown, A. and Hatch, M. (2003) 'Is ethnography jazz?', *Organization,* 10(1): 5–31.

Jack, G. and Westwood, R. (2009) *International and Cross-Cultural Management Studies: A Postcolonial Reading,* Basingstoke, Palgrave Macmillan.

Jankowicz, D. (2005) *Business Research Projects,* London, Thomson Learning.

Jensen, T., Sandström, J. and Helin, S. (2009) 'Corporate codes of ethics and the bending of moral space', *Organization,* 16(4): 529–545.

Jermier, J., Knights, D. and Nord, W. (eds) (1994) *Resistance and Power in Organizations,* New York, Routledge.

Johnsen, R. and Gudmand-Høyer, H. (2010) 'Lacan and the lack of humanity in HRM', *Organization,* May 17(3): 331–344.

Johnson, G. (1992) 'Managing strategic change – strategy, culture and action', *Long Range Planning*, 25(1): 28–36.

Johnson, G., Scholes, K. and Whittington, R. (2008) *Exploring Corporate Strategy: Text and Cases*, Harlow, Pearson Education Ltd.

Johnson, P. (2006) 'Where democracy?: A review and critique of the conceptual dimensions and implications of the business case for organizational democracy', 13(2): 245–274.

Jones, C. (2003) 'Theory after the postmodern condition', *Organization*, 10(3): 503–525.

Jones, C. (2004) 'Jacques Derrida' in Linstead, S. (ed.) *Organization Theory and Postmodern Thought*, London, Sage Publications.

Jones, C. (2007) 'Deconstructionism' in Clegg, S. and Bailey, J. (eds) *International Encyclopedia of Organization Studies*, London, Sage Publications.

Jones, C. (2009) 'Poststructuralism in critical management studies' in Alvesson, M. Bridgman, T. and Willmott, H. (eds) *Handbook of Critical Management Studies*, Oxford, Oxford University Press, pp. 76–98.

Jones, C. (2010) 'Derrida, business, ethics', special issue of *Business Ethics: A European Review*, 19(3): 235–237.

Jones, C. and Ten Bos, R. (eds) (2007) *Philosophy and Organization*, Abingdon, Routledge.

Jones, C., Parker, M. and Ten Bos, R. (2005) *For Business Ethics*, London, Routledge.

Jones, O. (2000) 'Scientific management, culture and control: A first-hand account of Taylorism in practice', *Human Relations*, 53(5): 631–653.

Kallinikos, J. (2009) 'On the computational rendition of reality: Artifacts and human agency', *Organization*, 16(2): 183–202.

Kärreman, D. and Alvesson, M. (2009) 'Resisting resistance: Counter-resistance, consent and compliance in a consultancy firm', *Human Relations*, 62(8): 1115–1144.

Kavanagh, D. (2009) 'Institutional heterogeneity and change: The university as fool', *Organization*, 16(4): 575–595.

Kavanagh, D., Kuhling, C. and Keohane, K. (2008) 'Dance-work: Images of organization in Irish dance', *Organization*, 15(5): 725–742.

Keenoy, T. and Seijo, G. (2010) 'Re-imaging email: Academics in the castle', *Organization*, March 17(2): 257–282.

Kelley, E., Mills, A. and Cooke, B. (2006) 'Management as a Cold War phenomenon?', *Human Relations (Special Issue – The Cold War and Management)*, May 59(5): 603–610.

Kerr, R. and Robinson, S. (2009) 'The hysteresis effect as creative adaptation of the Habitus: Dissent and transition to the "corporate" in the post-soviet Ukraine', *Organization*, 16(6): 829–853.

Kim, J., MacDuffie, J.P. and Pil, F. (2010) 'Employee voice and organizational performance: Team versus representative influence', *Human Relations*, 63(3): 371–394.

Kirkpatrick, I. and Ackroyd, S. (2003) 'Archetype theory and the changing professional organization: A critique and alternative', *Organization*, 10(4): 731–750.

Kitay, J. and Wright, C. (2007) 'From prophets to profits: The occupational rhetoric of management consultants', *Human Relations*, 60(11): 1613–1640.

Knights, D. (2002) Writing Organizational Analysis into Foucault, *Organization*, l9(4): 575–593.

Knights, D. (2004) Michel Foucault in Linstead, S. (ed.) *Organization Theory and Postmodern Thought*, London, Sage Publications.

Knights, D. and Willmott, H. (1999) *Management Lives: Power and Identity in Work Organizations*, London, Sage Publications.

Knights, D. and Willmott, H. (2000) *The Re-engineering Revolution: Critical Studies of Corporate Change*, London, Sage Publications.

Knights, D. and Willmott, H. (2007) *Introducing Organizational Behaviour and Management*, London, Thomson Learning.

Koch, M. (2006) *Roads to Post-Fordism: Labour Markets and Social Structures in Europe*, Aldershot, Ashgate Publishing Limited.

Kociatkiewicz, J. and Kostera, M. (2010) 'Exclusion and denial within experience economy', *Organization*, March 17(2): 257–282.

Kolb, D.A. (1983) *Experiential Learning: Learning as the Source of Learning and Development*, London, Prentice Hall.

Kolb, D.A. and Fry, R. (1975) 'Towards an applied theory of experiential learning' in Cooper, C. (ed.) *Theories of Group Process*, London, Wiley, pp. 33–58.

Korczynski, M. (2003) 'Communities of coping: Collective emotional labour in service work', *Organization*, 10(1): 55–79.

Korczynski, M. (2005) 'The point of selling: Capitalism, consumption and selling', *Organization*, 12(1): 69–88.

Kotler, P. (1972) 'A Generic concept of marketing', *Journal of Marketing*, April 36: 46–54.

Kotler, P. and Levy, S. (1969) 'Broadening the concept of marketing', *Journal of Marketing*, January 33: 10–15.

Kuhn, T. (1970) *The Structure of Scientific Revolutions*, Chicago, University of Chicago Press.

Kuhn, T. (2009) 'Positioning lawyers: Discursive resources, professional ethics and identification', *Organization*, 16(5): 681–704.

Latour, B. (1987) *Science in Action*, Milton Keynes, Open University Press.

Law, J. and Singleton, V. (2005) 'Object lessons', *Organization*, 12(3): 331–355.

Lawrence, T. (2004) 'Rituals and resistance: Membership dynamics in professional fields', *Human Relations*, 57(2): 115–143.

Lawrence, T. and Phillips, N. (2004) 'From Moby Dick to Free Willy: Macro-cultural discourse and institutional entrepreneurship in emerging institutional fields', *Organization*, 11(5): 689–711.

Learmouth, M. (2008) 'Speaking out: Evidence-based management – A backlash against pluralism in organization studies?', *Organization*, 15(2): 283–291.

Learmouth, M. (2009) ' "Girls" working together without "teams": How to avoid the colonization of management language', *Human Relations*, 62(12): 1887–1906.

Leca, B. and Naccache, P. (2006) 'A critical realist approach to institutional entrepreneurship', *Organization*, 13(5): 627–651.

Letiche, H. (2006) 'Critical management studies (not) in the Netherlands', *Critical Perspectives on International Business*, 2(3): 172–182.

Lincoln, Y. and Guba, E. (1985) *Naturalistic Enquiry*, Thousand Oaks, Sage Publications.

Linstead, S. (ed.) (2004) *Organization Theory and Postmodern Thought*, London, Sage Publications.

Linstead, S. and Allison, P. (2006) Gender as multiplicity: Desire, displacement, difference and dispersion', *Human Relations*, 59(9): 1287–1310.

Linstead, S. and Brewis, J. (2007) 'Passion, knowledge and motivation: Ontologies of desire', *Organization*, 14(3): 351–371.

Linstead, S. and Hopfl, H. (2000) *The Aesthetics of Organization*, London, Sage Publications.

Linstead, S. and Linstead, A. (2005) *Thinking Organization*, London, Routledge.

Linstead, S. and Pullen, A. (2006) 'Gender as multiplicity: Desire, displacement, difference and dispersion', *Human Relations*, 59(9): 1287–1310.

Linstead, S., Fulop, L. and Lilley, S. (2009) *Management and Organization: A Critical Text*, Basingstoke, Palgrave Macmillan.

Lipovetsky, G. and Charles, S. (2005) *Hypermodern Times*, Cambridge, Polity Press.

Llewellyn, N. and Harrison, A. (2007) 'Reply: Politics dressed as plain truth (again): On rhetorics of "openness" and "impartiality" in Christensen et al.', *Human Relations*, 60(4): 663–672.

Lukes, S. (1974) *Power: A Radical View*, London, Macmillan.

Lyotard, F. (1979) *The Postmodern Condition: A Report on Knowledge*, Paris, Editions de Minuit.

Mack, K. (2008) 'Sense of seascapes: Aesthetics and the passion for knowledge', *Organization*, 14(3): 373–390.

Malpas, S. and Wake, P. (2006) *The Routledge Companion to Critical Theory*, London, Routledge.

Marcuse, H. (1991) *One Dimensional Man*, London, Routledge.

Marens, R. (2010) 'Destroying the village to save it: Corporate social responsibility, labour relations and the rise and fall of American hegemony', *Organization*, pending 17(6): 743–766.

Martens, W. (2006) 'The distinctions within organizations: Luhmann from a cultural perspective', *Organization*, 13(1): 83–108.

Marx, K. (1867/1967) *Capital*, New York, International Publishers.

Massumi, B. (ed.) (2002) *A Shock to Thought: Expression After Deleuze and Guattari*, London, Routledge.

Matanle, P., McCann, L. and Ashmore, D. (2008) 'Men under pressure: Representations of the "Salaryman" and his organization in the Japanese Manga', *Organization*, 15(5): 639–664.

Maylor, H. and Blackmon, K. (2005) *Researching Business and Management*, Basingstoke, Palgrave Macmillan.

McCabe, D. (2007) 'Individualization at work?: Subjectivity, teamworking and anti-unionism', *Organization*, 14(2): 243–266.

McCabe, D. (2010) 'Strategy as power: Ambiguity, contradiction and the exercise of power in a UK building society', *Organization*, March 17(2): 151–175.

McKinlay, A. (2002) ' "Dead selves": The birth of the modern career', *Organization*, 9(4): 595–614.

McLoughlin, I. and Badham, R. (2005) 'Political process perspectives on organization and technological change', *Human Relations*, 58(7): 827–843.

McPhee, R. (2004) 'Text, agency and organization in the light of structuration theory', *Organization*, 11(3): 355–371.

Mescher, S., Benschop, Y. and Dooreward, H. (2010) 'Representations of work: Life balance support', *Human Relations*, 63(1): 21–39.

Miettinen, R. and Virkkunen, J. (2005) 'Epistemic objects, artefacts and organizational change', *Organization*, 12(3): 437–456.

Milgram, S. (1974) *Obedience to Authority*, New York, Harper and Row.

Miller, D. (2001) *Consumption: Critical Concepts in the Social Sciences*, London, Routledge.

Mills, A., Mills, H. and Thomas, K. (2004) *Identity Politics at Work: Resisting Gender, Gendering Resistance*, London, Routledge.

Minahan, S. and Wolfram-Cox, J. (2007) *The Aesthetic Turn in Management*, Farnham, Ashgate, July.

Misheva, V. (2004) 'The cold war within a sociological systems perspective', *Kybernetes*, 35(3/4): 286–307.

Morgan, G. (1997) *Images of Organization*, London, Sage Publications.

Mueller, F. and Carter, C. (2005) 'The "HRM Project" and managerialism: Or why some discourses are more equal than others', *Journal of Organizational Change Management*, 18(4): 369–382.

Munro, I. (2004) *Information Warfare in Business: Strategies of Control and Resistance in the Network Society*, London, Routledge.

Munro, I. (2010) 'Defending the network organization: An analysis of information warfare with reference to Heidegger', *Organization*, 17(2): 199–222.

Murgia, A. and Poggio, B. (2009) 'Challenging hegemonic masculinities: Men's stories on gender culture in organizations', *Organization*, 16(3): 407–423.

Mutch, A. (2003) 'Communities of practice and habitus: A critique', *Organization Studies*, 24(3): 383–401.

Mutch, A. (2005) 'Discussion of Willmott: Critical realism, agency and discourse – moving the debate forward', *Organization*, 12(5): 781–786.

Nayak, A. and Beckett, A. (2008) 'Infantilized adults or confident consumers?: Enterprise discourse in the UK retail banking industry', *Organization*, 15(3): 407–425.

Newell, S., Robertson, M. and Swan, J. (eds) (2001) Management fads and fashions *Organization*, 8(1): 5–15.

Nonaka, I., and Takeuchi, H. (1995) *The Knowledge Creating Company: How Japanese Companies Create the Dynamics of Innovation*, Oxford, Oxford University Press.

Noon, M. and Blyton, P. (2006) *The Realities of Work*, Basingstoke, Palgrave Macmillan.

O'Connor, E. (1999) 'Minding the workers: The meaning of "Human" and "Human Relations" in Elton Mayo', *Organization*, 6(2): 223–246.

O'Doherty, D. (2008) 'The blur sensation: Shadows of the future', *Organization*, 15(4): 535–561.

Ogber, J. (2000) 'Mythicizing and reification in entrepreneurial discourse: Ideology-critique of entrepreneurial studies', *Journal of Management Studies*, 37(5): 605–635.

Orwell, G. (1949) *Nineteen Eighty Four*, London, Secker and Warburg.

Packard, V. (1960) *The Hidden Persuaders*, Harmondsworth, Penguin.

Park, C. and Keil, M. (2009) 'Organizational silence and whistle-blowing on IT projects: An integrated model', *Decision Sciences*, November 40(4): 901–918.

Parker, M. (1995) 'Critique in the name of what: Postmodernism and Critical approaches to organization', *Organization Studies*, 16(4): 553–564.

Parker, M. (1997) 'Organizations and citizenship', *Organization*, 4(1): 75–92.

Parker, M. (2000) *Organizational Culture and Identity*, London, Sage Publications.

Parker, M. (2002a) *Against Management*, Oxford, Polity.

Parker, M. (2002b) *Utopia and Organization*, Oxford, Blackwell.

Parker, M. (2003) 'Introduction: Ethics, politics and organizing', *Organization*, 10(2): 223–248.

Parker, M. (2008) 'Eating with the Mafia: Belonging and violence', *Human Relations*, 61(7): 989–1006.

Parker, M., Fournier, V. and Reedy, P. (2007) *The Dictionary of Alternatives: Utopianism and Organization*, London, Zed Books.

Paulsen, N. and Hernes, T. (eds) (2003) *Managing Boundaries in Organizations – Multiple Perspectives*, Houndmills, Palgrave Macmillan.

Peci, A. (2009) 'Taylorism in the socialism that really existed', *Organization*, 16(2): 289–301.

Perrow, C. (2008) 'Conservative radicalism', *Organization*, 15(6): 915–921.

Phillips, M. and Rippin, A. (2010) 'Howard and the mermaid: Abjection and the Starbucks' foundation memoir', *Organization*, 17(4): 481–499.

Phillips, N. (2006) 'The adolescence of critical management studies: A postscript to Clegg, Kornberger, Carter and Rhodes', *Management Learning*, 37(1): 29–31.

Pina e Cunha, M. (2004) 'Organizational time: A dialectical view', *Organization*, 11(2): 271–296.

Polkinghorne, D. (1988) *Narrative Knowing and the Human Sciences,* Albany, State University of New York Press.

Quack, S. (2007) 'Legal professionals and transnational law-making: A case of distributed law agency', *Organization,* 14(5): 643–666.

Reed, M. (2005) 'Reflections on the realist turn in organization and management studies', *British Journal of Management Studies,* 42(8): 1621–1644.

Rehn, A. (2008) 'Speaking out: On meta-ideology and moralization – a prolegomena to a critique of management studies', *Organization,* 15(4): 598–609.

Rhodes, C. and Brown, A. (2005) 'Writing responsibly: Narrative fiction and organization studies', *Organization,* 12(4): 467–491.

Rhodes, C. and Parker, M. (2008) 'Images of organizing in popular culture', *Organization,* 15(5): 627–637.

Rhodes, C. and Westwood, R. (2008) *Critical Perspectives of Work and Organization in Popular Culture,* London, Routledge.

Riach, K. (2007) ' "Othering" older worker identity in recruitment', *Human Relations,* 60(11): 1701–1726.

Riad, S. (2008) 'Organization's engagement with ancient Egypt: Framing and claiming the sublime', *Organization,* 15(4): 475–512.

Ricouer, P. (1984) *Time and Narrative (Vol 1),* Chicago, University of Chicago Press.

Ritzer, G. (1993) *The McDonaldization of Society,* London, Pine Forge Press.

Roberts, J. (2005) 'The power of the "imaginary" in the disciplinary processes', *Organization,* 12(5): 619–642.

Robertson, M. and Swan, J. (2004) 'Going public: The emergence and effects of soft-bureaucracy within a knowledge-intensive firm', *Organization,* 11(1): 123–148.

Robertson, P. (2003) 'Organization space/time: From imperfect panopticon to hetrotopian understanding', *Ephemera,* 3(2): 126–132.

Robinson, S. and Kerr, R. (2009) 'The symbolic violence of leadership: A critical hermeneutic study of leadership and succession in a British organization in the post-Soviet context', *Human Relations,* 62(6): 875–903.

Rosenfeld, P., Giacalone, R. and Riordan, C. (2002) *Impression Management: Building and Enhancing Reputation at Work,* London, Thomson Learning.

Rosenthal, P. and Peccei, R. (2006) 'The social construction of clients by service agents in reformed welfare administration', *Human Relations,* 59(12): 1633–1658.

Rowlinson, M. and Carter, C. (2002) 'Foucault and history in organization studies', *Organization,* 9(4): 527–547.

Said, E. (1978) *Orientalism,* London, Vintage Books.

Salaman, G. and Storey, J. (2008) 'Understanding enterprise', *Organization,* 15(3): 315–323.

Samra-Fredericks, D. (2005) 'Strategic practice, "discourse" and everyday interactional constitution of "power effects" ', *Organization,* 12(6): 803–841.

Santana, M. and Carpentier, N. (2009) 'Mapping the rhizome: Organizational and informational networks of two Brussels alternative radio stations', *Telematics and Informatics,* 27(2): 162–176.

Scarbrough, H., Buelens, M. and Willem, D. (2007a) 'Impact of coherent versus multiple identities on knowledge integration', *Journal of Information Science,* 32: 1–31.

Scarbrough, H., Swan, J., Robertson, M. and Nicolini, D. (2007b) 'Introduction special issue on organizational learning knowledge and capabilities', *Management Learning,* 38: 259–265.

Seidl, D. (2007) 'Standard setting and following in corporate governance: An observation-theoretical study of the effectiveness of governance codes', *Organization,* 14(5): 705–727.

Sewell, G. (1998) 'The discipline of teams: The control of team-based industrial work through electronic and peer surveillance', *Administrative Science Quarterly*, 43: 406–469.

Sewell, G. (2005) 'Nice Work?: Rethinking managerial control in an era of knowledge work', *Organization*, 12(5): 685–704.

Sewell, G. and Wilkinson, A. (1992) 'Someone to watch over me: Surveillance discipline and the Just-in-time labour process', *Sociology*, 26(2): 271–289.

Sikka, P. (2009) 'Financial crisis and the silence of the auditors', *Accounting, Organizations and Society*, 34(6–7): 868–873.

Sikka, P. and Hampton, H. (2005) 'The role of accountancy firms in tax avoidance: Some evidence and issues', *Accounting Forum*, 29(3): 325–343.

Sikka, P. and Willmott, H. (2010) 'The dark side of transfer pricing: Its role in tax avoidance and wealth retentiveness', *Critical Perspectives on Accounting*, 21(4): 342–356.

Sikka, P., Haslam, C., Kyriacou, O. and Agrizzi, D. (2007) 'A rejoinder to professionalizing claims and the state of UK professional accounting education: Some evidence', *Accounting Education*, 16(1): 59–64.

Sillince, J. and Brown, A. (2009) 'Multiple organizational identities and legitimacy: The rhetoric of police websites', *Human Relations*, 62(12): 1829–1856.

Silverman, D. (2010) *Qualitative Research*, London, Sage Publications.

Sim, S. and Van Loon, B. (2005) *Introducing Critical Theory*, Royston, Icon Books Ltd.

Simpson, R. and Lewis, P. (2005) 'An investigation of silence and a scrutiny of transparency: Re-examining gender in organization literature through the concepts of voice and visibility', *Human Relations*, 58(10): 1253–1275.

Sims, D. (2003) 'Between the millstone: A narrative account of the vulnerability of middle managers' storying', *Human Relations*, 56(10): 1195–1211.

Sims, D., Pullen, A. and Beech, N. (2007) *Exploring Identity: Concepts and Methods*, Basingstoke, Palgrave Macmillan.

Sköld, D. (2009) 'An evil king "thing": Rising, falling and multiplying in trucker culture', *Organization*, 16(2): 249–266.

Sköld, D. (2010) 'The other side of enjoyment: Short circuiting marketing and creativity in the experience economy', *Organization*, 17(3): 363–378.

Slack, T. and Hinings, C. (2004) 'The pace, sequence and linearity of radical change', *Academy of Management Journal*, 47(1): 15–39.

Slutskaya, N. and De Cock, C. (2008) 'The body dances: Carnival dance and organization', *Organization*, 15(6): 851–868.

Spender, J. and Scherer, A. (2007) 'The philosophical foundation of knowledge management: Editors' introduction', *Organization*, 14(1): 5–28.

Spicer, A., Alvesson, M. and Kärreman, D. (2009) 'Critical performativity: The unfinished business of critical management studies', *Human Relations*, 62(4): 537–560.

Stein, H. (2001) *Nothing Personal, Just Business: A Guided Journey into Organizational Darkness*, Westport, Quorum Books.

Stokes, P. and Gabriel, Y. (2010) 'Engaging with genocide: The challenge for organization and management studies', *Organization*, 17(5): 461–480.

Stookey, S. (2008) 'The future of critical management studies: Populism and elitism', *Organization*, 15(6): 922–924.

Strati, A. (1992) 'Aesthetic understanding of life', *Academy of Management Review*, 17(3): 568–581.

Strati, A. (1998) 'Organizational symbolism as a social construction: A perspective from the sociology of knowledge', *Human Relations*, 51(11): 1379–1402.

Sturdy, A., Clark, T., Fincham, R. and Handley, K. (2009) 'Between innovation and legitimation – Boundaries and knowledge flow in management consultancy', *Organization*, 16(5): 627–653.

Sturdy, A., Grugulis, I. and Willmott, H. (eds) (2001) *Customer Service: Empowerment and Entrapment*, Basingstoke, Palgrave Macmillan.

Tadajewski, M. (2009a) 'The debate that won't die? Values incommensurability, antagonism and theory choice', *Organization*, 16(4): 467–485.

Tadajewski, M. (2009b) 'Editing the history of marketing thought', *Journal of Historical Research in Marketing*, 1(2): 318–329.

Tadajewski, M. and Jones, D.G.B. (eds) (2008a) *The History of Marketing Thought*, Volume I, London, Sage Publications.

Tadajewski, M. and Jones, D.G.B. (eds) (2008b) *The History of Marketing Thought*, Volume II, London, Sage Publications.

Tadajewski, M. and Jones, D.G.B. (eds) (2008c) *The History of Marketing Thought*, Volume III, London, Sage Publications.

Taylor, J. and Robichaud, D. (2004) 'Finding the organization in the communication: Discourse as action and sensemaking', *Organization*, 11(3): 393–413.

Ten Bos, R. (2005) 'On the possibility of formless life: Agamben's politics of gesture', *Ephemera*, 5(1): 26–44.

Thanem, T. (2006) 'Living on the edge: Towards a monstrous organization theory', *Organization*, 13(2): 163–193.

Thomas, R. and Davies, A. (2005) 'What have the feminists done for us? Feminist theory and organizational resistance', *Organization*, 12(5): 711–740.

Thomas, R. and Linstead, A. (2002) 'Losing the plot?: Middle managers and identity', *Organization*, 9(1): 71–93.

Thompson, P. (1993) 'Postmodernism: Fatal distraction' in Hassard, J. and Parker, M. (eds) *Postmodernism and Organizations*, London, Sage Publication.

Thompson, P. and McHugh, D. (2009) *Work Organizations: A Critical Approach*, Basingstoke, Palgrave Macmillan.

Tietze, S., Cohen, L. and Musson, G. (2003) *Understanding Organizations Through Langauge*, London, Sage Publications.

Tiffin, J. and Terashima, N. (2001) *Hyperreality: Paradigm for the Third Millennium*, London, Routledge.

Tinker, T. and Carter, C. (2003) 'Spectres of accounting: Contradictions or conflicts of interest?' *Organization*, 10(3): 577–582.

Tomlinson, F. and Schwabenland, C. (2010) 'Reconciling competing discourses of diversity? The UK non-profit sector between social justice and the business case', *Organization*, 17(1): 101–121.

Townley, B. (2002) 'Managing in modernity', *Organization*, 9(4): 549–574.

Townley, B. (2005) 'Discussion of Roberts: Controlling Foucault', *Organization*, 12(5): 643–648.

Tsoukas, H. (1998) 'Introduction: Chaos, complexity and organization theory', *Organization*, 5(3): 291–313.

Turner, V. (1969) *The Ritual Process*, Penguin, Harmondsworth.

Urry, J. (2002) *The Tourist Gaze*, London, Sage Publications.

Van Maanen, J. (1988) *Tales of the Field: On Writing Ethnography*, Chicago, University of Chicago Press.

Van Maanen, J. (1991) 'The smile factory: Work at Disneyland' in Frost, P., Moore, L., Louis, M., Lundberg, C. and Martin, J. (eds) *Reframing Organizational Culture*, Newbury Park, Sage Publications.

Vattimo, G. (1997) *Beyond Interpretation: The Meaning of Hermeneutics for Philosophy*, Cambridge, Polity Press.

Voronov, M. (2008) 'Towards engaged critical management studies', *Organization*, 15(6): 939–945.

Waddington, D. (2004) 'Participant observation' in Cassell, C. and Symon, G. (eds) *Essential Guide to Qualitative Methods in Organizational Research*, London, Sage Publications, pp. 165–179.

Wagner-Tsukamoto, S. and Tadajewski, M (2006) 'Cognitive anthropology, bricolage and the problem solving behaviour of green consumers', *Journal of Consumer Behaviour: An International Review*, 5(3): 235–244.

Wajcman, J. (1998) *Managing Like a Man: Women and Men in Corporate Management*, Cambridge, Polity Press.

Warhurst, C. and Nickson, D. (2007) 'A new labour aristocracy? Aesthetic labour and routine interactive service', *Work, Employment, Society*, 21(4): 785–798.

Warhurst, C., Grugulis, I. and Keep, P. (2004) *Skills That Matter*, London, Macmillan Press.

Watson, T. (1994) *In Search of Management: Culture, Chaos and Control in Managerial Work*, London, Routledge.

Watson, T. (2006) *Organising and Managing Work*, Harlow, Prentice-Hall.

Watson, T. (2008) *Organising and Managing Work*, Harlow, Pearson Education Ltd.

Watson, T. (2009) 'Narrative, life story and manager identity: A case study in autobiographical identity work', *Human Relations*, 62(3): 425–452.

Watson, T. and Harris, P. (1999) *The Emergent Manager*, London, Sage Publications.

Weber, M. (1947) *The Theory of Social and Economic Organization*, New York, Free Press.

Weber, M. (1958) *The Protestant Ethic and the Spirit of Capitalism*, New York, Charles Scribner and Sons.

Weick, K. (1995) *Sensemaking in Organizations*, London, Sage Publications.

Westwood, R. and Rhodes, C. (2006) *Humour, Work and Organization*, London, Routledge.

Whitley, R. (2003) 'From the search for universal correlations to the institutional structuring of economic organization and change: The development and future of organization studies', *Organization*, 10(3): 481–501.

Whittle, A. (2008) 'From flexibility to work-life balance: Exploring the changing discourses of management consultants', *Organization*, 15(4): 513–534.

Willmott, H. (1995) 'Managing the academics: Commodification and control in the development of university education in the U.K.', *Human Relations*, 48(9): 993–1027.

Willmott, H. (2005) 'Theorizing contemporary control: Some poststructuralist responses to some critical realist questions', *Organization*, 2(5): 747–780.

Willmott, H. (2006) 'Pushing at an open door: Mystifying the CMS manifesto', *Management Learning*, 37(1): 33–37.

Willmott, H. (2008) 'Critical management and global justice', *Organization*, 15(6): 927–931.

Willmott, H. (2009) 'Commentary: Science as intervention – recasting Weber's moral vision', *Organization*: 16(1): 143–153.

Willmott, H. (2010) 'Creating "value" beyond the point of production: Branding, financialization and market capitalization', *Organization*, 17(5): 517–542.

Winiecki, D. (2009) 'The call centre and its many players', *Organization*, 16(5): 705–731.

Wisser, M. (2010) 'Critical management studies and "mainstream" organization science: A proposal for a rapprochement', *International Journal of Organizational Analysis*, 18(4): 466–478.

Witz, A., Warhurst, C. and Nickson, D. (2003) 'The labour of aesthetics and the aesthetic organization', *Organization*, 10(1): 33–54.

Wolf, N. (1990) *The Beauty Myth*, London, Chatto and Windus.

Woźniak, A. (2010) 'The dream that caused reality: The place of the Lacanian subject of science in the field of organization', *Organization*, May 17(3): 395–411.

Wray-Bliss, E. (2002) 'Abstract ethics, embodied ethics: the strange marriage of Foucault and positivism in LPT', *Organization*, 9(1): 5–39.

Wray-Bliss, E. (2004) 'The right to respond? The monopolisation of "Voice" in CMS', *Ephemera*, 4(2): 101–120.

Wray-Bliss, E. and Brewis, J. (2008) ''Re-searching ethics: Towards a more reflexive critical management studies', *Organization Studies*, 29(12): 1521–1540.

Zanoni, P., Janssens, M., Benschop, Y. and Nkomo, S. (2010) 'Unpacking diversity, grasping inequality: Rethinking difference through critical perspectives', *Organization*, 17(1): 9–29.

Zhang, Z., Spicer, A. and Hancock, P. (2008) 'Hyper-organizational space in the work of J.G. Ballard', *Organization*, 15(6): 889–910.

Index